HIDDEN HISTORY *of* JACKSON COUNTY, MICHIGAN

Linda Hass

Published by The History Press
Charleston, SC
www.historypress.com

Front cover: The Barbershop & Bathroom of Edward M. Stoeckle, complete with a traditional barber pole. Taken near downtown Jackson around 1900. *Courtesy Jackson District Library*.

First published 2020

Manufactured in the United States

ISBN 9781467145787

Library of Congress Control Number: 2020934427

Contents

Contents

Preface

The history of Jackson County, Michigan, is an expansive topic, from the ancient glaciers that carved our rolling countryside to the modern buildings that comprise our urban landscape. Textbooks and headlines present only part of the picture. Thousands of noteworthy stories have never been told. Others were told but were overshadowed by bigger headlines. Still others made headlines but deserve a fresh look.

The *Hidden History of Jackson County, Michigan* treats readers to some of these bypassed or long-forgotten stories of people, places and events in the county. It takes readers on a historical adventure, from the time a prehistoric giant got trapped in a muddy pool in what is today Tompkins Township, to an elaborate dance hall suspended above Clark Lake in the early to mid-1900s. Some of the stories shed new light on familiar figures, including extraordinary people who fell from grace. Other stories highlight unsung heroes who contributed to Jackson in countless ways—tales of ordinary people who rose to extraordinary challenges.

Readers will be introduced to noble figures, including the former enslaved American who founded a church that thrives to this day, the feisty farmer who defied a southern posse, the invisible unsung patriarch who helped mold Jackson and settlers who regularly drove wolves from their paths as they walked to church.

History fans will learn about colorful characters like the last French fur trapper, the prestigious businessman who murdered his mother in cold blood, radical newspaper editors who launched antislavery crusades, brazen bank robbers who traumatized a small town and the multiple crossed paths of Civil War enemies with ties to Grass Lake.

The book will venture down a few secret trails, such as the hush-hush visit of Eleanor Roosevelt to Summit Township, the hidden compartment used by an Underground Railroad activist and the unearthing of giant, prehistoric bones.

Intriguing landmarks and locations also will be explored, including the casino that went up and came down in a blaze of glory; the true birthplace of the Republican Party; the starting point for every boundary in the state of Michigan; and the haunt of mobsters, musicians and possibly ghosts in Blackman Township.

To gather evidence for this book, I've camped in Jackson County's libraries and museums, prevailed on curators and reference librarians, scanned hundreds of microfilmed newspapers, tromped through countless cemeteries with my husband (who has an uncanny ability to locate obscure tombstones) and explored dusty archives throughout the state. To distinguish between the credible and the non-credible, priority was given to primary evidence backed by corroborating secondary evidence. There are no single-source stories presented in this book.

The Hidden History of Jackson County, Michigan is not intended to present a comprehensive chronicle of Jackson County's history. Other books have done that. This rendition takes a closer look behind the scenes, illustrated by vintage photographs, postcards and sketches. All historical markers, parks, buildings and landmarks mentioned are publicly accessible. Stories represent all of Jackson County's nineteen townships, providing a little something for everyone.

Turn the page, dive into *The Hidden History of Jackson County, Michigan* and explore local history as you never have before.

Acknowledgements

This book would not have been possible without the assistance and support of reference librarians. Calvin Battles, adult services coordinator at Jackson District Library's Carnegie branch, helped locate vital photos and Susan Panak, White Library archivist, Spring Arbor University, located documents and photos from Spring Arbor Township. Ken Wyatt and L. Talbott rendered invaluable historical and editorial services. The inspired sketches of Brianne Witt, assistant art professor, Spring Arbor University, made blurry photos of key historical figures come to life. The Marketing Machine Co. gave many of the historical figures a digital platform at jacksonmiundergroundrail.com. Deanda Johnson, Midwest regional manager for the National Underground Railroad Network to Freedom, provided inspiration for the story about Roswell Rexford. And Bobbi Rosenberg was a source of continual support.

I am grateful for the resources and permissions of the Detroit Public Library, Burton Historical Collection and the Bentley Historical Library, University of Michigan, Ann Arbor. I'm also grateful for the contribution of Jeff Davis, owner of Greater Lansing Monuments. Davis provided a headstone noting the Civil War service of Colonel Charles V. DeLand, one of Jackson's radical antislavery editors featured in this book. DeLand, who raised troops for the Civil War, was wounded many times, survived two prisoner of war camps and was ultimately breveted to brigadier general of the U.S. Volunteers in recognition of his "gallant and meritorious service." Sadly, his grave was unheralded for 119 years. In 2019, Davis generously

The grave of Civil War hero Charles V. DeLand at Mt. Evergreen Cemetery in Jackson lacked military acknowledgement until 2019. *Author's photo.*

responded to my request for a grave marker honoring DeLand's military service, and Kelli Hoover, director of the City of Jackson Parks, Recreation, Cemeteries & Trails Department, authorized the cement pad.

Last but not least, I thank my family for tolerating a history-obsessed member. My husband, Ed, renders unfailing technical support during PowerPoint presentations and has put up with a wife whose idea of a good time is tromping through cemeteries and exploring dusty archives. Thanks also to my son, Jason, and mother, Ann, for their unswerving support.

Part I

EARLY JACKSON

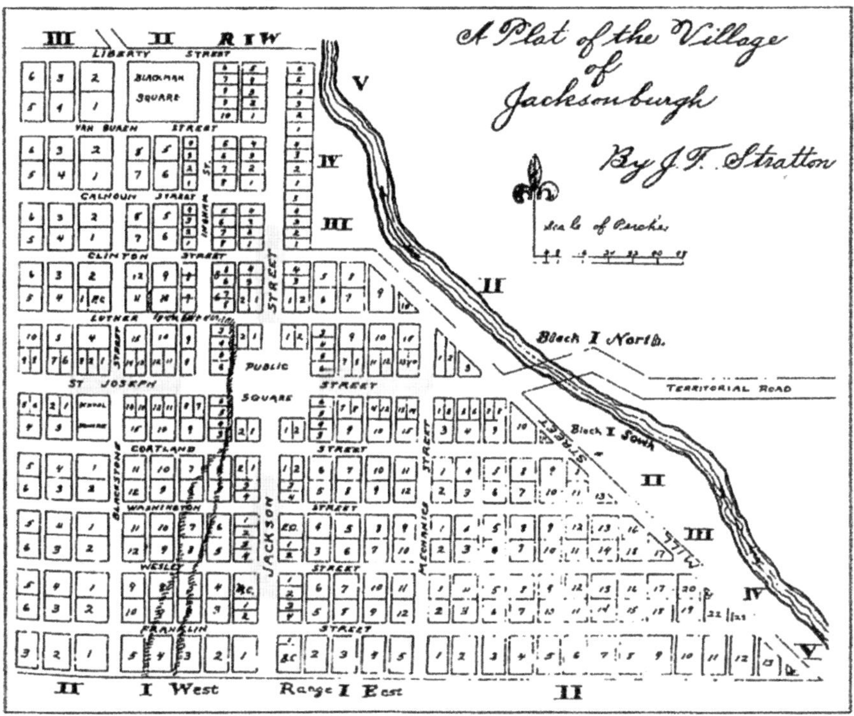

The plat of the Village of Jacksonburgh revolves around the public square, Jackson's historic center. *Courtesy Jackson District Library.*

I

Pewytum and the Washtenong Sepe

Most Jackson residents have heard of Horace Blackman (1801–1850), the town's celebrated founder. They may not know, however, that long before Blackman arrived, the place they call "home" had been home to Native Americans who helped make Blackman's claim possible.

Hints of this heritage exist on a bronze plaque at the intersection of West Trail and North Jackson Streets. The memorial, affixed to a large rock, shows where "Horace Blackman, with Captain Alex Laverty and the Indian guide Pe-wy-tum camped the night of July 3, 1829." This date, according to the plaque, marks "the founding of the City of Jackson."

Between the lines on the plaque is an intriguing backstory marked by the convergence of Native American trails and indigenous people in a landscape filled with rippling blue streams, verdant forests, silvery birch and plentiful game. It is a story too long to fit on a marker but too fascinating to ignore.

The tale begins with a prospective settler from New York named Horace Blackman, who read mixed reviews about the beguiling Michigan Territory. Some reports condemned the area as a thinly populated wasteland. Others praised its benefits, including streams that could sustain mills and fertile land ripe for crops. Which report was true? The curious explorer decided to see for himself. Blackman hired Alexander Laverty, an experienced woodsman, and Pewytum, a Native American guide, to lead him to a remote location in the south-central part of what would become the state of Michigan.

Heading out from the frontier hamlet of Ann Arbor (the farthest western outpost from Detroit at the time), the adventurers reached their destination

Left: Jackson founder Horace Blackman first camped in this spot (West Trail and North Jackson Streets) in 1829. *Author's photo.*

Right: In 1829, Horace Blackman registered a claim for 160 acres in what would become Jackson at two dollars per acre. *Courtesy Jackson District Library.*

after a hot, two-day hike. Their target was the east bank of a river that Native Americans called the Washtenong Sepe, or "clear, swift stream running over a bed of pebbles." Today, this stream is known by its shorter and less descriptive name: the Grand River. The men forded the stream approximately where Trail Street crosses the river and camped the night of July 3 on the west bank near what is now downtown Jackson.

The next day, the Fourth of July, the threesome awoke from their riverbank encampment to survey the land before them. The misty morning light illuminated Native American cornfields to the north, confirming the soil's fruitfulness. To the south were dense forests that could supply lumber for building and fuel. To top it off, a drinkable stream gurgled under their noses. Blackman discovered another asset not mentioned in any report: several trails intersected the river, suggesting the area's potential as a major trading thoroughfare.

Blackman decided that his firsthand impressions confirmed the positive reports. This was the place the plucky pioneer would call home. The men feted the occasion with an impromptu celebration. Traces of their celebration are long gone, but if nature could replay the sights and sounds it has absorbed over the millennia, curious ears would hear a rousing rifle salute that echoed far and wide. They would also hear the first bilingual speech ever uttered in

Jackson. Laverty honored the occasion with discourse in Potawatomie, the language of the dominant indigenous group, and in English.

Afterward, the men toasted the day with a cool drink of water from the Washtenong Sepe. Pewytum capped off the ceremony with one last rifle shot. The gunfire attracted curious natives who came to see what the commotion was all about. The two groups ended up celebrating the occasion with a feast of game, potatoes, fresh fish and roasted corn.

Blackman returned to Ann Arbor and then walked to Monroe, where he registered his claim for 160 acres in what is now Jackson, at two dollars per acre. On February 6, 1831, Governor Lewis Cass fulfilled Blackman's hopes by declaring "Jacksonburg" the county seat. Thus began the chain of events that would lead to the growth and development of Jackson County.

Helping to make these milestones possible were indigenous trails leading to this spot in 1829; the Native American Pewytum, who guided explorers here; and a first-ever celebratory feast uniting Native Americans and Jackson's adventuresome founder—facts long forgotten but fascinating, nonetheless.

FUN FACTS

- Horace and his brother Russel Blackman cleared their new property and built the first log cabin ever erected in Jackson on the corner of what is now Ingham and Trail Streets.
- In 1830, Blackman's claim was named Jacksonburg in honor of then-president Andrew Jackson. Postal officials changed the name to Jacksonopolis to avoid confusion with other Jacksonburgs. In 1838, townspeople shortened the name to Jackson. The Village of Jackson was incorporated in 1843. In 1857, Jackson became a city.
- In 1847, Jackson was a contender for the state capitol, which was then located in Detroit. Ultimately, legislators chose Lansing (which at the time had only a dam and one log cabin) over Jackson, which was a bustling town of about three thousand and the fourth largest in the state.
- Dominant industries in Jackson in the nineteenth century included coal mining, corset making and railroading. Local car companies included the Briscoe Motor Company and Jackson Automobile Company, which produced the Jaxon steam car.[1]

2

THE INVISIBLE PATRIARCH

There is no park, statue or township named after Jackson pioneer William R. DeLand (1794–1876). But this unsung hero did more to promote Jackson's earliest growth than any other individual, making him a vital, if invisible, mover and shaker in Jackson's development.

William was among the first settlers to occupy the original log cabin built in Jackson. He was also among the first surveyors of the area, the first justice of the peace and the force behind a Jackson publishing dynasty. In addition, he cofounded one of Jackson's earliest churches, and he and his wife, Mary DeLand, were leading participants in the Underground Railroad, a secret network that transported enslaved Americans from the South to the North in the early to mid-1800s.

Oddly, these contributions are little acknowledged today. While his cousin, Horace Blackman, has a township and a park named after him (even though Blackman left the village of Jackson after six years), no such honor has ever been bestowed on William, who remained in Jackson for the rest of his life to help the town grow and prosper. It is a strange epitaph for a patriarch who contributed so much.

William's story begins in North Brookfield, Massachusetts, where he and Mary lived and where he worked as a schoolteacher. He was well established in the town, but he had an adventurous heart. When cousin Horace asked if he would be willing to move to the untamed wilderness of the Michigan Territory, he listened with an open mind.

William, a visionary who always seemed to be on the cutting edge of trends, saw the potential of such a move. He had witnessed the beauty and

Left: William DeLand founded Jackson's first newspaper, the *Jacksonburg Sentinel*, among other contributions. *Sketch by Brianne Witt, assistant art professor, Spring Arbor University, courtesy Linda Hass.*

Right: Mary DeLand influenced her family to participate in the Underground Railroad. *Sketch by Brianne Witt, assistant art professor, Spring Arbor University, courtesy Linda Hass.*

bounty of Michigan firsthand when he joined a surveying party that came to this state before Blackman and his band of explorers ever set foot in the area. He had seen the rolling landscapes carpeted in green, waded through the cool, fresh streams and heard the howling wildlife—a testament to plentiful game. With that positive experience in mind, William accepted his cousin's offer.

On April 14, 1830, seven years before Michigan became a state, William, Mary and their two small children loaded their possessions in a covered wagon, painted the word *Michigan* on the wagon's side and lumbered west, traveling forty miles a day. On Sunday, May 28, the wagon reached its destination.

Women and men perceived their new home quite differently, with the men gravitating toward a flattering description, calling it a "goodly land, flowing with milk and wild honey, and plenty of venison into the bargain." The women were less than amused at their first accommodations, a rough-hewn log cabin with a dirt floor and one large room that was shared communally. That first night, Mary and the other women dutifully prepared and served

The DeLand homestead was a safe house in Jackson's Underground Railroad. *Courtesy Burton Historical Collection, Detroit Public Library.*

the first meal and then these refined ladies went out behind the house and had a "good cry."

As Jackson developed, William rose quickly through the ranks and was appointed justice of the peace. He was elected county clerk and later probate judge, an office he held for eight years. With these positions came prosperity and a larger home on the northeast corner of Mechanic and Franklin Streets. The stately white home with covered porches served as a station on the Underground Railroad for many years. It also served as a silent witness to the tender hearts of a couple who felt a deep responsibility to help the enslaved.

After decades of guiding Jackson's growth and development, William died on November 26, 1876, and was buried at Jackson's Mt. Evergreen Cemetery. His obituary stated, "He was one of the first to carry the surveyor's chain…wrote the first notice…rendered the first decision in law, and formed the first religious society here."

Unfortunately, he is rarely, if ever, credited when village founders are honored. His name, however, is briefly listed among Underground Railroad activists on a Michigan historical marker in Mt. Evergreen Cemetery. Nearby, the inscription on his family's granite grave monument proclaims that the DeLands were a "Pioneer Family of Jackson." What it does not proclaim is equally true: this pioneer stood out among Jackson's patriarchs. He may be unfamiliar today, but he was indispensable to the founding of the town Jacksonians call home.[2]

3
Jackson's Radical Newspapers

By 1837, Jacksonburg boasted a post office, a courthouse, a primitive schoolhouse and a cluster of businesses. One thing the rustic village lacked was a newspaper. To remedy this glaring omission and to help bring civilization to the small burg, William DeLand and Norman Allen led the charge in recruiting a printer and a press. Their quest resulted in a Vermont printer, Nicholas Sullivan, moving to Jackson and setting up shop in the public square. One of the reasons that Nicholas moved was because his brother, Reverend William Sullivan, who lived in Jacksonburg, offered to help him in the venture. The fruit of their labor was the village's first newspaper, the *Jacksonburg Sentinel*, first printed in 1837. The Ramage press provided by the village was previously used by Michigan's first newspaper, the *Detroit Gazette*.

Jacksonburg Sentinel

The *Jacksonburg Sentinel* was generally published on Saturdays, beginning in 1837. Its office was on the second floor of a ramshackle wooden building "at the northeast corner of Jackson Street and the public square." (Today Bucky Harris Park.) A yearly subscription cost two dollars in advance.

Production in those days was slow. The clunky wooden press could only print one page at a time, requiring four impressions to publish one issue

Jacksonburg Sentinel.

"Reason is Man's distinguishing attribute--freedom of speech his inalienable birthright--the liberty of the Press his impregnable safeguard."

BY N. SULLIVAN. JACKSONBURG, MICHIGAN: [illegible], 1837. VOL. 1.---NO. 6.

THE
Jacksonburg Sentinel
WILL BE ISSUED EVERY SATURDAY MORNING.

Office, on the north-east corner of Jackson street and the Public Square.

TERMS.—Two dollars in advance, (payable on the receipt of the first number;) Two dollars and fifty cents, within six months; and Three dollars if not paid until the expiration of the year.

☞ADVERTISEMENTS not exceeding one square, will be inserted three times for one dollar. A liberal discount made to those who advertise by the year.

POETICAL.

[*From the Saturday Courier.*]
HOPE FADETH AWAY.
[BY THE MILFORD BARD.]

Away delusive dream of joy,
Vain meteor of the mind;
Thou art but fancy's gilded toy,
That floats upon the wind.

Even as the lightning's lurid light
'Lumines yon clouds, that roll,
So art thou for a moment bright,
Within the human soul.

But when the lightning's glare expires,
Midnight doth hold her reign;
So when the fickle flame retires,
The soul is dark again.

I saw a brilliant bubble rest
Upon a silvery stream;
Floating upon the billow's breast,—
'Twas like hope's fairy dream.

savages, headed by the notorious renegado Simon Girty.—Knowing the weakness of the force opposed to the assailants, and anxious also to share in the perils and glories of the battle, he resolved to hasten to the assistance of the settlers. Taking with him a few choice volunteers, the little party mounted their horses, and moved at a rapid pace towards Wheeling. It was their intention to approach the fort secretly, under cover of the woods and undergrowth, and to ascertain at what particular point the besiegers were stationed. Then gaining an opposite position, by a well known signal, the major was to inform those within the fort of the arrival of succor, and by a rapid movement hoped to secure the admittance of the party. Fortune favored the design of the hunters; they approached the fort in an opposite direction from the principal point of attack; the signal was given, and all the party save M'Colloch, succeeded in entering the stockade. The major being in the rear of the body, was thwarted in his purpose by a band of Indians hitherto concealed, who sprang from the thicket and placed themselves before him. Fully appreciating the value of such a prisoner as M'Colloch, they withheld their fire, raised a shout, and sprang towards him with the apparent intention of taking him alive, in order to afford them an opportunity of wreaking their vengeance, by compelling him to undergo that horrid course of torture adopted by the savages, which is more terrible than death itself. On perceiving his perilous situation, the hunter turned the head of his horse and bounced through the thickets towards the top of the towring hill that overlooks the fort; once having gained its summit, he hoped to be able to avail himself of a passage on the ridge, and by the superior fleetness of his steed, to distance this pursuit of his enemies. Swiftly did his gal-

From the Marshall Times.

No person who has lived long among the native Indians of our country, and been familiar with their customs and manners their strong natural attachments and greatness of soul, can but feel an interest in their welfare.

A miserable remnant of the tribe of the Putawatomies yet remain among us.—They are disgusting in their appearance, and extremely filthy; and it is not until habit has rendered their presence familiar, that a new comer can be reconciled to have them about him. Their language is peculiar to their tribe, and as a general rule, they will take no pains to learn the English; and unless necessity compels them, they will not speak what they do know of it. The whites buy their venison, [illegible], furs, [illegible], [illegible]berries, and such articles of [illegible] as they obtain in the wilds of the country, but in their intercourse with them, they are jealous and fearful that they will not be sufficiently paid for their articles of traffic.—They are generally indolent, and but few of them care for any thing more than enough to supply present necessity.

Preparations are making for their removal to the west. Those with whom I have had conversation on the subject, express an unwillingness to go away from the home of their birth, where they have from their childhood hunted the wild deer, or ensnared the smaller animals on the banks of the streams, or the margin of the lakes, for their covering of fur; and if they finally reluctantly consent to go, they will yet say that soon they will come back, and having embodied all their tribes, they will then force the white man to retreat back again, they will hunt their own deer in their own long-loved wilds, which they have inherited from their forefathers, from generation to generation. X.

THE AMERICAN PRESS.—From a "Lecture on Printing," delivered before the Portsmouth Lyceum, by C. W. Brewster, we glean the following facts, which exhibit in a striking light, the importance of the public press in the United States, and its immense power for good or for evil:

The first paper issued in the (then) British colonies was the Boston News Letter, commenced in 1704; the Boston Gazette followed in 1719; and the American Weekly Mercury was commenced in Philadelphia the same year. Previous to the Revolution, there had been seventy-eight different newspapers printed, of which only thirty-nine were then issued; and of these, only eight remain. Since that era, the number of papers has been constantly augmenting. "There are now about one thousand two hundred newspapers established in the United States, from which are issued, at a moderate calculation, one hundred million printed sheets annually; which, in one continuous sheet, would reach four times from pole to pole, and if embodied in a book form, would be equal to issuing six volumes as large as the Bible, every minute in the year."

Incredible as the above statement may appear to some, it is doubtless strictly true. In the Temperance office at Albany, there are constantly employed six steam and six hand presses: these throw off twenty copies of temperance documents, during each working minute of the year: no wonder, then, at the immense moral influence which the N. Y. State Society wields!

The Harpers, of New-York, employ one hundred and forty workmen and publish a volume of the Family Library size, every day in the year. The Fessendens, of Brattleborough, Vt., keep in operation seven or eight power presses, printing not far from twenty thousand sheets per day. At one end of their establishment is a paper

MOST [illegible].—We [illegible] recollect ever to have read of more deliberate murder than that detailed below. Why not give the name of the cold-blooded scoundrel who commanded the Wisconsin, that he may be known and shunned by every friend of humanity? The Chicago Advertiser says:

"We learn from a gentleman, (JAMES KINZIE, Esq. of this city,) who has just ascended the Illinois river, that a most melancholy occurrence took place, on Saturday the 18th inst. at about five miles from its mouth, where, through the obstinacy of the captains of two steamboats, one of their boats was sunk, the lives of all the deck passengers, amounting to more than twenty, lost, and the freight and baggage entirely destroyed.

"The captain of the *Wisconsin*, which was then ascending the river, had repeatedly stated that if he should meet the *Tiskilwa*, and her captain would not give him a clear channel, he should run her down. This, it seemed, provoked the captain of the other boat, and he became as obstinately determined not to turn out of his course. Both boats met at about five o'clock in the morning, at a time when all the passengers were in bed, and steered directly for each other till within a distance of only a few rods, when the captain of the Tiskilwa endeavored, but too late, to avoid the concussion; and turning a little out of the direct course, thus gave a fair broadside to the ascending boat, which took her just behind the wheel, and she sunk in less than three minutes after she was struck. The first notice of their extreme danger which the cabin passengers received, was the screams of those below, who were drowning; and without even time to put on their clothes, they merely escaped by jumping through the windows of the cabin, which, fortunately for them, had been completely

The *Jacksonburg Sentinel*, founded in 1837 by Underground Railroad activists, was Jackson's first newspaper. *Courtesy Jackson District Library.*

of the four-page *Sentinel*. Ink was spread with buckskin balls "the size of a dinner plate." Nicholas's young apprentice was William DeLand's son, Charles DeLand, who fondly recalled his days as an apprentice, a position called a printer's devil.

Charles wrote, "A man and a good stout boy could print about 100 copies in an hour. But it was quite a neat and tidy looking paper, and the people were all proud of it." The *Sentinel* was published for several years, although there were some lapses due to funding shortages. The next paper to use the Ramage press was the *American Freeman.*

AMERICAN FREEMAN

There has been some confusion over the location of Michigan's first abolition newspaper. It was not Ann Arbor, as has been claimed. Nor was it Detroit, another likely candidate. No, the first such paper in the state was printed in Jackson by radical preacher Reverend William Sullivan from the same wooden building as the *Sentinel* in 1838 or 1839.

The paper's prospectus, signed by William and dated March 6, 1839, left no doubt about its calling: "The *American Freeman* will be...an uncompromising supporter of the doctrines of the American Anti-Slavery Society...it will call on every voter to cast his suffrages in favor of the bleeding slave, and employ every civil privilege for his speedy emancipation."

The *Freeman* was filled with extracts from state and national organizations, such as the American Anti-Slavery Society and the Michigan Anti-Slavery Society. It also included excerpts from other papers and news of local meetings, such as the Young People's Temperance Society of Jackson.

The earliest extant issue of the *Freeman* was Vol. 1, No. 2, printed May 21, 1839, and the last issue was Vol. 1, No. 4, printed August 13, 1839. Despite its short run, the paper was a noble first effort and an important springboard to its longer-running successor, the *Michigan Freeman*, published by Jackson resident and Underground Railroad agent Seymour Treadwell.

MICHIGAN FREEMAN

The *Michigan Freeman* was initially published by the executive committee of the Michigan State Anti-Slavery Society and edited by Seymour Treadwell. It was printed weekly from the fall of 1839 to the fall of 1840. Unlike his predecessors, New York native Seymour Treadwell brought his own press and printer to Jackson.

Where did Treadwell set up that press? There is no question that it was in Jackson, but where specifically? Most historians place the *Michigan Freeman* in the public square because it was ultimately printed by Nicholas Sullivan, who was there, and because the preceding and subsequent papers were all located in the square—the center of commercial activity in the village.

The paper's exclusive mission to promote abolition was reflected in its inaugural issue on September 25, 1839: "To utterly and forever abolish the great moral and political evil and danger of slavery in the land." Typical content included antislavery convention proceedings, political speeches, excerpts from other papers, local meeting announcements and advertisements ranging from blacksmiths to mortgage sales.

Unfortunately, the *Michigan Freeman* also faced financial problems. The last extant issue of the *Michigan Freeman* was dated November 10, 1840. The next publication to take up the antislavery cause in Michigan was the *Signal*

MICHIGAN FREEMAN

"We hold these truths to be self-evident, that all men are created equal; that they are endowed by their Creator with certain inalienable ri[ghts] ... liberty, and the pursuit of happiness."—DECLARATION OF AMERICAN INDEPENDENCE.

S. B. Treadwell, Editor.] JACKSON, WEDNESDAY, SEPTEMBER 25, 1839.

THE MICHIGAN FREEMAN, is published every Wednesday morning, in Jackson, Jackson County, Michigan, *by the Executive Committee of the Michigan State Anti-Slavery Society.*

M. S. MOORE,
PUBLISHING AGENT AND PRINTER.

TERMS.

$2 per annum, *in advance*; $2 50 within *three* months; or $3 if payment be delayed *six months, in all cases.* Subscriptions paid within *one month* after receiving the first number, will be considered in advance.

Any person who will forward us $10 shall be entitled to a sixth copy gratis. $15, in advance, will pay for NINE copies, if sent to one post office.

one, desirous to hold a subject of such moment, in just estimation, will cast this humble sheet aside with perhaps a mere "*railing accusation!*"

In the course of our discussions, we shall amply disprove the unjust imputations so often cast upon the devoted friends of impartial liberty, that they are acting in violation of the spirit or the letter of the Constitution.—So far from this, we shall clearly show that they are the only class of people in our country who are at this late day acting in entire accordance with the great and noble design in relation to Slavery, of the framers of that instrument—that is, that it was to "*establish justice, form a more perfect union*" and al-

have used those liberties to enslave so many whose arms were nerved, and whose breasts were bared in the common battle field. But as if to atone for the deed they had done, they at once went to work with their ample constitution in their hands to forever abolish all the slavery under its immediate jurisdiction, commencing with the great extent of country of all the North West Territory, now comprising Ohio, Indiana, Michigan, Illinois, Wisconsin, and Iowa. The perilous state of our own liberties at the present time, arising from the deep rooted and wide spread existence of Slavery in our country so hostile to all freedom, is solemnly teaching us the danger and the wickedness of the

how can you of this interest (Slavery) entertain apprehensions for your safety? What more do you claim? What more can you have? *How can those who hold power be oppressed by those who have none!*"

Who that perceives the constant truckling servility of the Northern National rival politicians for Slaveholding political favor, if he care nothing for the cruel enslavement of the millions of his fellow men, must not see this truly mortifying picture, & deeply feel himself humbled and degraded as an American.—But still there are many Northern political partisans through ignorance or interest meanly rivaling each other in courting Southern Slavery by abusing and *lynching* North-

The *Michigan Freeman*, founded in 1839 by Underground Railroad activists, was Michigan's second abolitionist newspaper. *Courtesy Bentley Historical Library, University of Michigan, Ann Arbor.*

of Liberty, published in Ann Arbor in April 1841. But the departure of the *Michigan Freeman* was not the end of an antislavery presence in Jackson's public square. The next local paper to grasp the antislavery baton was the *American Citizen*.

AMERICAN CITIZEN

The *American Citizen* was intended to be a general newspaper covering everything from local, state and national news to amusing short stories and advertisements. But it also consistently advanced an aggressive antislavery position.

The newspaper was founded on August 15, 1849, by partners A.A. Dorrance and Charles V. DeLand (son of William DeLand) and was originally published on the south side of the public square. Charles, an Underground Railroad activist, became the sole proprietor on October 16, 1850, and remained editor until September 1861.

Charles's passionate antislavery stance sparked public reactions ranging from supportive to antagonistic. On June 29, 1850, the *Citizen* fiercely criticized a southern newspaper's defense of slavery. About a week later, the *Citizen*'s office was set ablaze under mysterious circumstances. Commenting on the incident in the July 10, 1850 issue, Charles wrote, "We…regret the appearance of our paper this week; nevertheless, the indulgence of our

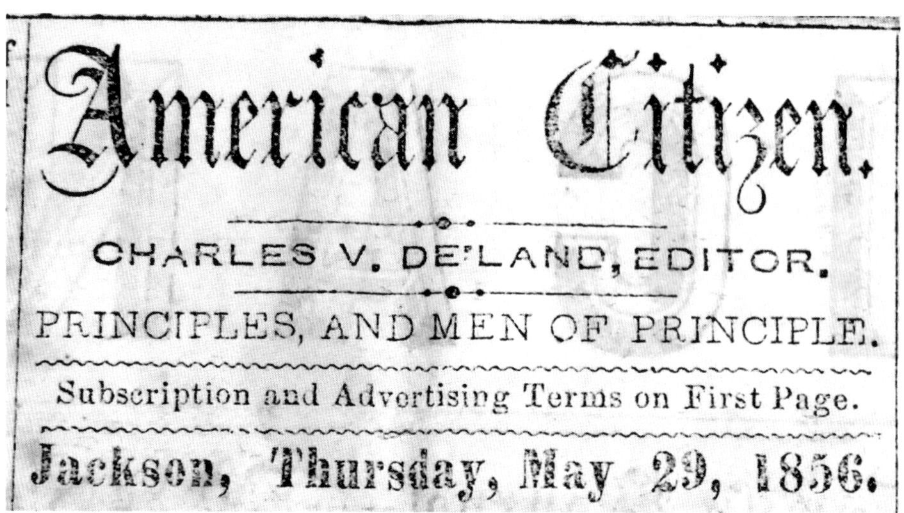
American Citizen.

CHARLES V. DE'LAND, EDITOR.

PRINCIPLES, AND MEN OF PRINCIPLE.

Subscription and Advertising Terms on First Page.

Jackson, Thursday, May 29, 1856.

The *American Citizen* newspaper office, founded in 1849, was firebombed twice. *Courtesy Bentley Historical Library, University of Michigan, Ann Arbor.*

patrons will be granted…could each one look upon the fragments of our office…we yet labor among the charred racks and melted fonts of type, within walls made dingy by the…conflagration…what is more unfortunate, the office is not insured for a single cent."

The fire, however, was no match for this firebrand, whose antislavery passion burned even hotter. Undeterred, Charles saved what he could, purchased what he could not salvage and published this blistering editorial a few weeks later: "They have passed the infamous Fugitive Slave Law, which not only robs the colored man of his freedom and himself at the same time, but it makes one great Hunting-Ground of the whole North, and Slave Hunters of her freeman. Fellow Citizens—Will you allow such principles as these to prevail in the country?"

After another broadside in December, history repeated itself, with a second fire mysteriously damaging the *Citizen*'s office. Once again, Charles regrouped, and on December 12, 1850, he penned an update: "The enterprising citizens of our town will…find fault with us in thus stopping our work, but our only reply is that if they are afraid of spontaneous combustion being the result of our occupancy of their buildings, they must be content to wait until a fireproof building can be erected."

Charles's provocative editorials culminated with an April 19, 1854 piece that took what had remained in the shadows—the Underground

Railroad—and blatantly exposed it to the light of day, openly referring to the secret network in Jackson. For abolitionist newspapers like the *Michigan Freeman*, such a column would not be unusual. But for a general newspaper to openly flout an otherwise secret network that operated in defiance of the law was nothing short of brazen.

THE *CITIZEN*'S ANTISLAVERY DRUMBEAT was echoed by newspapers throughout the state, culminating in a crescendo of editorials that some commentators said helped set public opinion and pave the way for the organization of the Republican Party. Today's readers can't be expected to remember the role Jackson's early newspapers played in launching an effective antislavery campaign. But long-forgotten newspaper articles testify to their impact, emerging from their dusty domain to live again and speak about the passion

RIVAL NEWSPAPERS

The nemesis of Charles DeLand, editor of the *American Citizen*, was Wilbur F. Storey, editor of the *Jackson Patriot*. Storey was so opposed to an antislavery sermon published in DeLand's newspaper that he left the First Congregational Church in a huff. Historians claim that the printed sermon was the match that lit Storey's incendiary opposition to abolition. Storey, who went on to become editor of the *Detroit Free Press* and the *Chicago Times*, routinely used his publishing platform to malign the DeLands and President Abraham Lincoln.

JACKSON, MICHIGAN. SUNDAY, AUGUST 20,

Citizen Patriot Predecessor Played Prominent Anti-Slavery Drive Role

Published City's First Extra on Lincoln's Death

BY ED F. SMITH

COL. C. V. DeLAND

State Wants VFW Parley

Moonshine Honor Out

American Citizen editor Charles V. DeLand fought slavery in the press and on the battlefield. *Courtesy Burton Historical Collection, Detroit Public Library.*

of a few overlooked radicals whose editorials helped rally the public behind the belief that all people are created equal. One of the leaders of this radical group was the *Citizen*'s irrepressible editor, Charles V. DeLand.

The historical significance of these early newspapers is confirmed on a Michigan historical marker installed in Bucky Harris Park in the summer of 2020. The cast-iron marker offers a teasing glimpse of the papers' contributions to the antislavery movement, including confirmation that the park was the site of Michigan's first abolitionist newspaper. But a marker can only say so much. Now readers know the fascinating stories behind the visionaries who founded these trailblazing papers.[3]

4
Pandemonium in the Pews

The First Congregational Church at 120 North Jackson Street stands at the intersection of North Jackson and Pearl Streets like a sturdy sentry flanked by two massive towers. The Romanesque Revival structure, dedicated on October 18, 1860, and still used today, is an island frozen in time amid a sea of modern structures. It's hard to believe this solid, stately church has such a volatile history, but it does.

Jackson's First Congregational Church traces its origins to 1837, when the Congregational and Presbyterian congregations formed a cooperative society. It was not a harmonious union. Unhappy with the proslavery action taken by the General Presbyterian Assembly and supported by several leading families, the Reverend Marcus Harrison, Jackson's first minister in the cooperative, rallied fifty-eight members to break away and form the First Congregational Church on March 6, 1841. The turmoil was a sign of things to come.

The fledgling congregation of the First Congregational Church met in a humble, wooden structure known as Session House at South Jackson and Washington Streets. Reverend Harrison's antislavery views generated so much antagonism that enemies stole a bell from the Session House and cut the mane and tail off Harrison's horse. When Harrison was warned about a plot to kill him, he hid for several days in an insect-filled swamp near Blackstone Street. Even that failed to deter the strong-willed pastor and his determined flock. The church was the first in Jackson County to pass a resolution condemning slavery.

As the congregation grew, it moved from the Session House to a building near the current location—a spot so hot in the summer that it was called the "pepper box." In 1845, the congregation built a structure on West Michigan Avenue and then almost lost it. A fire mysteriously ignited in a pile of straw under the pulpit of the empty church several hours after a temperance sermon. Providentially, the fire went out on its own, with little damage done.

The First Congregational Church, a Romanesque Revival structure in Jackson, was dedicated in 1860. It still holds services today. *Author's photo.*

By 1858, the burgeoning membership of 226 needed more space to congregate, so the church bought two lots at the present site, 120 North Jackson Street. The next year, they hired renowned architect Horatio N. White of Syracuse, New York, to design the Romanesque Revival structure. Construction of the Congregational church began that year. The orange brick building, distinguished by semicircular arches, decorative arcading and colorful stained-glass windows, was dedicated on October 18, 1860. In September 1861, soldiers from the Jackson Greys and Jackson County Rifles gathered with their wives and families in the sanctuary for a special service before departing for the Civil War.

Throughout the church's history, a host of firebrand pastors have left their marks on the local community, including Reverend Gustavius Foster, who shepherded the First Congregational Church from the 1840s until the mid-1850s. He was at the helm when the Fugitive Slave Law was passed by the United States Congress on September 18, 1850. To say the law did not sit well with the congregation would be an understatement. For many, the law, which required northerners to assist southerners in hunting escaped slaves or face punishment, was a gross violation of moral standards and civil rights.

On October 13, 1850, Reverend Foster preached a sermon on "The Doctrine of Subjection to 'the Powers that be' in its Application to the Fugitive Slave Law." The scripture, based on Titus 3:1, was controversial enough in itself, but applied to the recent provocative law, it ignited a firestorm. Reverend Foster held nothing back. He began by expounding on the conditions under which Christians are obligated to follow the civil law and then posed the rhetorical question: "Where then is the limit?" His answer, printed in all capital letters, followed: "JUST WHERE ITS REQUIREMENTS CLASH WITH THE REQUISITIONS OF GOD."

On October 16, 1850, editor Charles V. DeLand printed the entire sermon in the *American Citizen* newspaper. The discourse became a rallying cry for an antislavery movement that gained momentum and moral legitimacy, thanks, in part, to this church's trailblazing founders and pastors.[4]

5
The Changing Community

The roots of Jackson's ethnic diversity began with historic push-pull factors that are nearly forgotten today. These forces, pushing groups from their native lands and attracting them to Jackson, formed the very building blocks of Jackson's current demographics.

The first foreign-born people to settle in Jackson were the Irish, who arrived in the 1830s to help build the prison. Their presence was one of the factors that prompted the establishment of the first local Catholic mission in 1836. The mission ultimately evolved into the first Catholic church, built in 1857. Today, St. John the Evangelist Church is located at 711 North Martin Luther King Jr. Drive.

The first Jews to move to Jackson included Jacob Hirsch, Jacob Levy and Bernard Wolff, who emigrated from Germany in the 1840s. They purchased an acre of land for a burial ground on North West Avenue in 1859 and opened the first Jewish synagogue in the city, Temple Beth Israel, around 1862. Today, the synagogue is located at 801 West Michigan Avenue and is known for its colorful glass windows, among other distinctions. Temple Beth Israel Cemetery, which was placed on the National Register of Historic Places in 2009, is Michigan's second-oldest extant Jewish cemetery.

Many Germans arrived in the 1860s, pushed from their homelands by famine and war and attracted by ample opportunities for work due to labor shortages during the Civil War (1861–65). Polish immigration to Jackson began in the early 1870s. Most Polish families lived on the east side of

St. John the Evangelist Church, established in 1857, was the first Catholic church in Jackson. *Courtesy Jackson District Library.*

St. Demetrius Orthodox Church, Jackson, is adorned with Byzantine frescos that were painted using a technique that is over one thousand years old. *Author's photo.*

town, near their jobs on the railroads and in factories. By 1876, one-fifth of Jackson's population was foreign born. By 1910, Germans and Poles were among the largest foreign-born groups in the city.

Immigration from eastern European countries began in the early 1900s. William Georgeopolis was the first Greek to settle in Jackson, opening a shoe shining business around 1901. Other eastern European groups soon followed, including Macedonians, who established many restaurants.

Jackson's African American community began in the early 1830s, with Thomas Trist (also spelled Tryst), who opened a blacksmith shop on the west side of Jackson Street near Louis Glick Highway. Another milestone was the construction of Jackson's first African American church in 1852. The African Methodist Episcopal Church at 218 East Franklin Street is still used today. The first African American elected to a county position was Frank Thurman, who served as coroner in 1880.

While the historic forces that brought these groups to Jackson no longer exist, many of the landmarks, businesses and traditions they established continue to enrich our county today. Examples range from paczkis,

JACKSON'S BELOVED BARBER

Richard Nichols, an enslaved American, escaped from a Virginia plantation around 1842. He arrived in Jackson with the clothes on his back and a pair of scissors—tools of his trade as a barber. Over the years, Nichols's skills and friendly personality endeared him to the town. When his former "master" attempted to take him back to Virginia around 1852, local abolitionists whisked Nichols to Canada. Enraged, the master threatened to sue Jackson's officials and track Nichols down again. "Excitement ran high and trouble was feared" until antislavery activists paid the Southerner "the value of his man." With freedom papers in hand, Nichols's supporters escorted him home. Nichols became the co-owner of a popular barbershop called Nichols & Smith on the north side of Main Street. This true tale of escape, near-recapture and triumphant return would be lost to time were it not for Nichols's obituary in the August 22, 1867 issue of the *American Citizen* newspaper, which reflected on the life of "Nick," Jackson's beloved barber.*

* American Citizen, August 22, 1867. For more on Nichols's story, see https://jacksonmiundergroundrailroad.com/the-evidence.

traditional Polish fare, to St. Demetrius Orthodox Church at 3043 Seymour Road, an Eastern Orthodox church known as the "Jewel of Jackson" and painted from floor to ceiling with Byzantine frescos created with a technique over one thousand years old.[5]

6
Freedom So Dearly Won

When the Civil War began in 1861, George W. Green (1835–1917) was in his twenties and laboring as a stonemason in Virginia. It is not known what Green, an enslaved American, thought of this conflict or its potential effect on his freedom. Did he ever stand under the stars, hands raised to the heavens, and pray for a Union victory? He must have held a glimmer of hope that such an outcome was possible.

Four years after the war began, that flicker burst into a bright reality when General Robert E. Lee surrendered his Confederate forces to Union general Ulysses S. Grant in Green's home state of Virginia. A new day had dawned for the nation's almost four million in bondage. It was a day of freedom but also a day of decision for the newly freed. What would Green do with his newfound independence? Although his response to this opportunity occurred more than 150 years ago, the consequences of his actions continue to affect Jackson residents today.

George and his wife, Sarah, also a former enslaved American, moved north shortly after the Civil War and ultimately settled in Jackson. But personal freedom was not enough for this couple—they wanted to exercise their right to worship publicly, so they held Baptist services in their humble cottage. It was a small step but a significant one that resulted in the founding of the first black Baptist church in Jackson—a church that exists to this day. The April 25, 1920 issue of the *Jackson Citizen Patriot* best sums up the creation of this groundbreaking congregation: "Shortly after the Civil War, Mr. and Mrs. George W. Green, two former slaves from

Left: In 1865, George Green, a former enslaved American, founded the Second Baptist Church (today Second Missionary Baptist Church) in Jackson. *Courtesy Second Missionary Baptist Church.*

Below: In 1910, the Second Baptist Church congregation posed outside its original church building for a group photo. *Courtesy Second Missionary Baptist Church.*

HISTORICAL CLAIMS TO FAME

Second Missionary Baptist Church at 304 East Prospect Street has several historical claims to fame. Not only was the sesquicentennial church founded by former enslaved Americans George and Sarah Green in 1865, but it also produced one of the longest-serving pastors in Jackson County's history. The late Reverend Amos Polk Williams, who served as pastor for fifty-eight years, was honored for this milestone by his church and by the community in 2012.

the South, came to Jackson and made their home in a little three-room cottage on what is now West Pearl Street...where the first services of the colored Baptist faith were ever held....It was a service of thanksgiving to the Almighty for their freedom from bondage, a freedom so dearly won... soon there was quite a thriving congregation...the church was organized as the Second Baptist Church of Jackson."

As the congregation grew, it purchased a lot on 208 East Franklin Street in 1870 and built a small, wood-framed structure on the property. George served as deacon of the church, which hosted various pastors who often preached without pay. On weekdays, George worked as a stonemason to feed the couple's eight children. Given his occupation, those same strong hands also likely labored to help construct the house of worship during the evenings.

In 1892, George and another resident successfully ran for the office of county coroner—a two-year term filled by two residents. When the popular resident was reelected in 1894, the newspaper said he and his partner had "nearly 2,000 majority apiece, so many that nobody had time to figure it out."

Around 1910, the Greens moved to a farm in Summit Township. According to the U.S. census that year, George was listed as a "farmer" and an "employer" on land he owned. The census also indicated that he could read and write, both of which were incredible accomplishments for someone likely forbidden from acquiring an education or owning land in the slave South. That same year, the congregation constructed a white masonry church on the same lot—an occasion marked by a dated cornerstone and a group photo.

George died in his Summit Township home in 1917. He was laid to rest at Jackson's Mt. Evergreen Cemetery at section 26, lot 10. Sarah died in 1921 and was buried beside George at the same cemetery. In 1972, the growing congregation, now called the Second Missionary Baptist Church, constructed a new house of worship at 304 East Prospect Street. The spacious tan brick building continues to serve the community in many ways, although few Jackson residents outside the church are aware of the congregation's amazing backstory. What might the Greens have said if they could foresee that their first steps of faith would result in such an enduring legacy? We will never know, of course, but they likely would have been pleased to know that their freedom, so dearly won, led to a faith so strongly held.[6]

7

The Incompetent Criminal

If there was a contest for the most incompetent criminal ever, a Jacksonian would certainly vie for the title. This tragicomedy began on the evening of January 24, 1889, when an intruder broke into an upscale home on First Street and snuck upstairs where the homeowner, Mary Latimer, lay sleeping. The intruder shot her in the head twice with a .32-caliber revolver and departed without taking any valuables. Adding to the strangeness of the crime, the family dog gave no alarm. The following morning, a neighbor discovered Mrs. Latimer's blood-soaked body.

Jackson police chief John Boyle wasted no time heading the investigation into the slaying of one of Jackson's most prominent citizens. Mary's husband, Robert F. Latimer, was a highly respected druggist who died only fifteen months prior. After his death, Mary continued to reside in the family home with the couple's only child, Robert Irving Latimer (1865–1945). The dashing twenty-three-year-old businessman had inherited his father's drugstore and went by his middle name.

Where was Irving the night of the murder? That was the question Boyle asked Irving's clerk, who said his boss was in Detroit attending a funeral. Boyle decided to interrogate Irving in person. During the interview, Irving admitted he was not at a funeral after all. He had, in his own words, gone to Detroit for a rendezvous at the Griswold Hotel with a married woman named Trixie.

Irving's story didn't sit well with Boyle, and it's likely the name "Trixie" did nothing to add to its credibility, so Boyle questioned employees at the

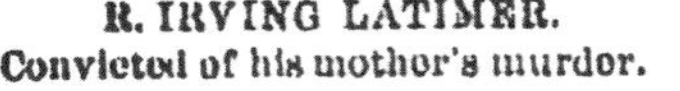

MARY H. LATIMER.
[From a Photograph taken in [illegible], the most recent in existence.]

Left: Prominent Jackson druggist R. Irving Latimer was convicted of matricide in 1889. *Taken from* Jackson Citizen Patriot *microfilm at the Jackson District Library.*

Right: Mary H. Latimer, mother of R. Irving Latimer, was murdered in her Jackson home. *Taken from* Jackson Citizen Patriot *microfilm at the Jackson District Library.*

Griswold Hotel. One person revealed that Irving had checked in but didn't spend the night in the hotel. Another had noticed blood on Irving's clothes the next day. Leaving no stone unturned, Boyle decided to question railroad employees, who said they saw Irving boarding a train from Detroit to Jackson around 10:10 p.m. Strangely, the following morning, he boarded another train from Jackson back to Detroit around 6:20 a.m.

If Irving was indeed the murderer, he wouldn't be so dumb as to leave the murder weapon in his office desk, would he? Returning to Jackson, Boyle found a .32-caliber gun in Irving's desk. Jackson's incompetent criminal was arrested shortly thereafter. On further questioning, Irving maintained that everything could be easily explained. What really happened was that when he didn't find Trixie at the Griswold Hotel, he returned to Jackson and found her waiting for him there. She later boarded a train out west. Irving spent the rest of the night in a cot in his office and then he took the morning train to Detroit to collect his bags, which were still at the Griswold Hotel.

A smart criminal might have gotten rid of bloody clothes. Irving, however, was not the sharpest tool in the shed, so when Boyle searched further, he found blood not only on Irving's coat but also on the bottom of his shoes and on his socks, which were soaked in blood. In short, Irving Latimer was busted. The resulting trial revealed that Irving was living way beyond his means, which left him little time for the pharmacy business that he had inherited. To pacify bill collectors, he had borrowed thousands of dollars from his mother, who conveniently died one week before the loan was due.

Adding to the tidal wave of evidence, the family dog's silence implied that the intruder was no stranger. A jury convicted Irving Latimer of murder on May 11, 1889, and sentenced him to life in prison in Jackson's state prison. For most convicts, that would be the end of the story, but this was Irving, after all.

One spring day, Jackson's incompetent criminal struck again. On March 26, 1893, Irving, who had been put in charge of the prison's drugstore, generously treated his guards to lemonade made from a secret Latimer family recipe. Apparently, he also had access to the prison's kitchen—and to lemons.

Did the guards smell a strange, pungent aroma mingling with citrus freshness when Irving handed them their drinks? Did they see unusual colors swirling in the glasses? We will never know, but shortly after

R. Irving Latimer, a prisoner in Jackson's Michigan State Prison, had access to the prison's drugstore and kitchen. *Courtesy Jackson District Library.*

TRIPLE MURDERER?

After R. Irving Latimer was returned to prison in 1889, it dawned on townsfolk that Irving's otherwise healthy father died under mysterious circumstances after drinking a glass of cider concocted by his son. This conveniently left Irving the sole inheritor of his father's West End Pharmacy. Irving had killed a prison guard, and a jury had already convicted Irving of killing his mother—did he kill his father too? It was too late to prove Irving's complicity in patricide, but townsfolk and newspapers thereafter referred to him as a triple murderer. In light of this, one would think he wouldn't want to be buried beside his parents, but truth is sometimes stranger than fiction. It is an overlooked but intriguing fact that Jackson's most infamous criminal was indeed buried next to his parents at block 2, range 3, lot 4, of Mt. Evergreen Cemetery.

imbibing this homemade concoction, one guard died and another became unconscious. At this point, Irving slipped out of his prison confines and back into the news.

A smart criminal might have developed a plan for his escape—perhaps something as elaborate as packing food. Irving, on the other hand, had no accomplices, no food and no plan. A few days later, a search party found him walking along the railroad tracks in Jerome, Michigan, starving and looking forlorn. Irving tried to persuade his captors that he was simply a hardworking railroad man heading home to his beloved family. But there was something that seemed suspicious—perhaps it was his prison garb as plain as day.

Jackson's most-wanted escapee was carted back to prison in a wagon and escorted into his old cell, where he proclaimed it was all a mistake. What really happened was that he accidently put too much of an old family ingredient into the lemonade. Anyone could have done it.

From that point on, Irving was denied parole or pardon until 1935, when he was pardoned by the governor. After his release, Irving went to work for the Ford Motor Company for a while but couldn't hold the job

SOUTHERN PRISON OF MICHIGAN

The Southern Prison of Michigan has several distinctions. It was Michigan's first state prison, built as a wooden fort on the north side of downtown in 1839. It housed thirty-five inmates inside makeshift wooden walls. By 1840, over eighty inmates were confined in the "Tamaracks," as it was called. After several prisoners escaped, the state replaced the wooden building with a brick, mortar and iron structure. By 1882, Jackson was home to the largest walled prison in the world, with over two thousand prisoners.

The Southern Prison of Michigan was completed in 1934 to replace the original facility. It held 5,700 cells and once again made Jackson the largest walled prison in the world. Reorganized in the 1980s, the prison now consists of four facilities, six cell blocks, 6,100 prisoners and 1,600 employees. Among its distinctions is the fact that, at one time, it was home to Jackson's ineptest criminal—R. Irving Latimer.*

Michigan's first state prison was located in Jackson in 1839. Today, the Southern Prison of Michigan houses over six thousand inmates. *Courtesy Jackson District Library.*

* *Jackson Citizen Patriot*, December 25, 1925; December 31, 1925; "Experience Jackson's Prison History," Experience Jackson.

and was ultimately committed to Eloise State Hospital, where he died at age eighty in 1945, thus ending the tragicomedy that was the life of Jackson's incompetent criminal.[7]

8
Birthplace of the Republican Party?

In the summer of 1854, discontent with existing political parties had reached a fever pitch. Many of Michigan's citizens hungered for a new entity that wielded the courage of its antislavery convictions. Jacksonians decided the time was ripe for action, so movers and shakers began preparations for a political convention in their hometown. *American Citizen* editor Charles DeLand sent one thousand announcements to counties, townships and newspapers throughout the state, inviting citizens "to assemble in mass convention on Thursday, the 6th of July at one o'clock, at Jackson."

The invitation had a dramatic result. At least five thousand, and as many as ten thousand, converged on the town from throughout the state, some arriving on horseback and others on foot. Whatever the number, the crowd overflowed Bronson Hall, the original venue, so the meeting was adjourned to an oak grove on the western outskirts of the town.

In this spot, described as "a beautiful piece of woods, situated on what was known as 'Morgan's Forty,'" an impromptu platform was prepared. There, speakers addressed a procession that stretched "as far back as the eye could reach....The scene...was an animated one...the Jackson brass band enlivening the occasion with patriotic airs," said one historian. Did this convention give birth to the Republican Party? To answer that question, let's examine the facts and the main competitor.

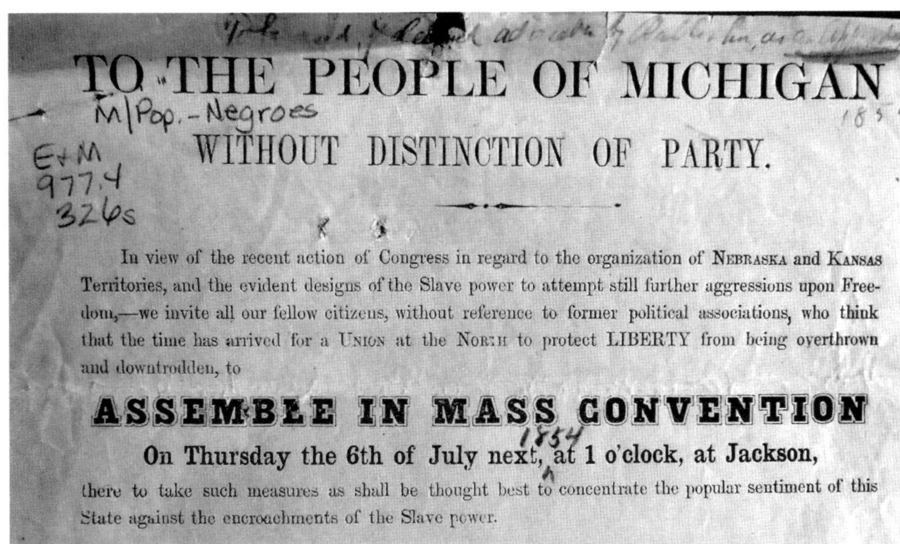

TO THE PEOPLE OF MICHIGAN

WITHOUT DISTINCTION OF PARTY.

In view of the recent action of Congress in regard to the organization of NEBRASKA and KANSAS Territories, and the evident designs of the Slave power to attempt still further aggressions upon Freedom,—we invite all our fellow citizens, without reference to former political associations, who think that the time has arrived for a UNION at the NORTH to protect LIBERTY from being overthrown and downtrodden, to

ASSEMBLE IN MASS CONVENTION

On Thursday the 6th of July next, at 1 o'clock, at Jackson,

there to take such measures as shall be thought best to concentrate the popular sentiment of this State against the encroachments of the Slave power.

Notices like this announced the mass convention that birthed the Republican Party in Jackson in 1854. *Courtesy Burton Historical Collection, Detroit Public Library.*

Jackson's Republican Convention, held under the oaks, drew thousands in 1854. *Courtesy Jackson District Library.*

Jackson's Oak Grove

Jackson's mass convention was guided by a sixteen-member committee that adjourned to a clump of oaks at the intersection of Franklin and Second Streets to prepare a platform. Their labors resulted in several resolutions, including two that called for the repeal of the Fugitive Slave Act and the Kansas-Nebraska Act, legislation that favored slavery.

The platform also promised to defend non-slaveholders in confrontations with slaveholders, nominated a slate of antislavery state candidates to represent these positions to an electorate and agreed on the name "Republican," among planks. Today, the event is memorialized by several historical markers in "Under the Oaks," a city park at the intersection of Franklin and Second Streets. An additional landmark, a bronze plaque affixed to a large boulder, states, "Here under the oaks July 6th 1854 was born the Republican Party destined in the throes of civil strife to abolish slavery, vindicate democracy, and perpetuate the Union."

In addition, several U.S. presidents have visited Jackson's site, acknowledging its "birthright" honors, including President Taft in 1910 and Eisenhower in 1952. This evidence seems to overwhelmingly support Jackson's claim to the birthplace of the Republican Party, but other towns have made similar assertions, most notably Ripon, Wisconsin.

Under the Oaks Park, at Franklin and Second Streets, marks the spot where the Republican Party was formed in Jackson in 1854. *Author's photo.*

This bronze plaque commemorates the birthplace of the Republican Party in Jackson on July 6, 1854. *Courtesy Jackson District Library.*

RIPON'S LITTLE WHITE SCHOOLHOUSE

Ripon, a small town about ninety miles north of Milwaukee, is acknowledged by many as the true birthplace of the Republican Party. In addition, Ripon's Little White Schoolhouse is listed on the National Register of Historic Places as the spot where the Republican Party was officially born in 1854. It is also recognized as such by the Republican National Committee.

Ripon's claim is based on a local gathering initiated by Alvan E. Bovay, a resident active in reform circles at the time. Disillusioned by existing parties that failed to curb slavery, Bovay gathered half the town's voters in its little schoolhouse on March 20, 1854. By night's end, the local committees of competing parties were dissolved, and "Republican," the term reportedly suggested by Bovay, was adopted as the new party's name, according to the town's application to the National Registry of Historic Places.

Wait a minute—doesn't Ripon's gathering predate Jackson's event? It sure does. Indeed, if one goes by chronology alone, Ripon's claim has the edge, and it certainly has the nod of the Republican National Committee. But if both towns claim birthright honors, which one is true, according to historical evidence?

Conflicting Evidence

Among primary evidence supporting Jackson's claim to the birthplace of the Republican Party are several contemporaneous newspaper reports and a detailed written account provided by an eyewitness who was an "active participant in the convention." Ironically, Ripon's application to the National Register of Historic Places states, "Contemporaneous records seem to be lacking with respect to that meeting and many others held afterward."

Bovay's gathering also lacks two essential qualifications of a viable political entity: a platform and candidates. Imagine trying to convince an American electorate that your meeting produced a national political party without offering any candidates to vote for, especially in a democracy. In this light, the gathering in Ripon seems more like the local expression of a concept than the birth of a viable party that bears such tangible qualities as a platform and candidates.

To top it off, Ripon's application to the National Register of Historic Places states, "In fairness to the Jackson assembly, it would seem that the elements of a party phenomenon: nominees for office, and adoption of a platform, committees, etc., are more clearly evident in the Jackson meeting." Wait, what? This affirmation of Jackson's claim is in *Ripon's* application to the National Registry of Historic Places? Yes, it is.

So why didn't authorities pick Jackson as the birthplace of the Republican Party? Records indicate Jackson's claim was rejected because the "original historic grove of oaks" is gone, and the "site's integrity is questionable." It's true—Jackson's site at the intersection of Franklin and Second Streets has a small park with historic markers and some mature oaks but not much more. An app was recently created, adding the site to a walking tour of historic landmarks in and around downtown Jackson. But as landmarks go, it is humble.

Since site integrity is so important to authorities, one would assume such integrity is present at the Wisconsin site. Well, not exactly. Ripon's application to the National Register of Historic Places states, "The original appearance of the schoolhouse is not known." It also states that the schoolhouse "has been relocated many times." In contrast, Jackson's site has remained constant and unmoved and does indeed contain several mature oaks—an appropriate feature for a park named Under the Oaks.

SPLIT THE DIFFERENCE

The puzzling and sometimes contradictory evidence regarding the birthplace of the Republican Party helps to explain the historic rivalry between Jackson and Ripon for birth honors. Where was the Republican Party *really* born? It is unlikely the issue will ever be resolved in a way that is mutually satisfying to either Ripon or Jackson, given their vested interests in tourism.

On the other hand, if something equitable were to be done, perhaps the towns could split the difference and give credit to each other? Jackson's claim could credit Ripon as taking early steps toward the conception of the party. Likewise, Ripon's claim could credit Jackson's convention for the actual birth of the party in terms of a tangible outcome (candidates, a platform, et cetera), with both towns contributing to a national movement in their own unique ways.

Or they could continue the historic rivalry, which is probably more likely.

FUN FACTS

- The term "Republican" was used by many people throughout the country, but most historians credit New York newspaper magnate Horace Greeley, not Ripon's Alvan Bovay, with coining the phrase.
- Regardless of which location gets credit for "birthing" the Republican Party (also referred to as the GOP or Grand Old Party), few dispute the party was founded in 1854, fueled by antislavery sentiment.
- In 1860, Republicans elected their first president, Abraham Lincoln, who historians generally credit as preserving the Union through his decision to fight rather than let the Southern states secede.[8]

9
The Greater Good

The roots of the Jackson District Library began with a small reading room and occasional lectures sponsored by a few men who formed a mutual improvement society in the mid-1800s. By 2018, those roots had blossomed into a public institution that circulated 1.8 million items throughout thirteen branches in Jackson County, among other services. Sandwiched between those two points is a fascinating backstory involving a wealthy industrialist, dedicated citizens and a strong-willed woman with a grand vision.

In 1854, however, grand visions were a remote possibility for a group of prominent businessmen who formed a mutual improvement society called the Young Men's Association (YMA). The YMA met in various public buildings, promoted literacy, hosted debates and sponsored lectures featuring celebrities like Ralph Waldo Emerson, P.T. Barnum and Mark Twain. In fact, an 1871 story in the *Jackson Weekly Citizen* noted, "An unusually fine audience assembled" to hear Twain, who spoke "in a nasal voice, which, from its twang was of itself amusing."

Association members had no idea their initiative would launch a major library system, but it appears they at least hoped it would. An announcement in the December 20, 1854 *American Citizen* newspaper stated, "The Young Men's Association of this Village are about raising funds for the purchase of a Public Library, and we presume the…citizens of our place will respond with their usual liberality.…We can conceive of no way in which to…secure a greater good to the community."

In 1864, YMA member William H. Withington advanced the cause by establishing a reading room on West Main Street (today West Michigan Avenue) that offered members twenty-one newspapers and four magazines. Among popular books of that era were *Uncle Tom's Cabin* by Harriet Beecher Stowe and *Walden: Life in the Woods* by Henry D. Thoreau. The room's popularity caught on, and in 1869, it incorporated under the laws of the state, offering up to 1,800 books.

In 1885, the state legislature passed an act allowing cities to levy taxes to support a free public library. Previously, the library was supported by a subscription fee of two dollars per year, plus other donations from interested citizens. Thanks to the new act, the Jackson Public Library was formed. For the first time, its resources were freely available to the entire community, including women, who no longer needed men to cosign for their library cards. Among popular books during this era was Mark Twain's recently published hit *The Adventures of Huckleberry Finn*.

From 1885 to 1900, the Jackson Public Library flourished. After shuffling its ever-expanding resources to various buildings, the library got a break in the early 1900s, when wealthy industrialist Andrew Carnegie began donating money to communities interested in building public libraries. The City of Jackson applied for some of these funds, and in 1901, it received

In 1906, supporters helped raise funds for the construction of the Jackson Public Library at West Michigan Avenue. *Courtesy Jackson District Library.*

The interior view of what is known as the Jackson District Library's Carnegie Library. *Courtesy Jackson District Library.*

$50,000 for the construction of a new library. There was only one problem: the building Jackson wanted to construct cost an additional $20,000.

In stepped Zelie P. Emerson, wife of successful Jackson businessman R.H. Emerson. Zelie, a petite powerhouse, knew Carnegie personally and persuaded the affluent industrialist to up the ante. She must have been persuasive. An agreement for the additional amount was signed in 1901, and the Carnegie Library (now known as the Jackson District Library's Carnegie Library) was opened to the public in 1906 with great celebration and fanfare.

In 1977, the library grew again when voters approved a tax to establish a single library system in the county that consolidated the Jackson Public Library and the Jackson County Library, a separate institution. The resulting combined system, the Jackson District Library, was created in 1978 to serve the entire county. In 1979, the Carnegie Library, which serves as the main branch, was designated a state historical site, and in 1980, it was recognized as a national historical site.

The humble origin of this community treasure is not apparent today. The modest reading room of 1854 is dwarfed by a library that, in 2018, served over sixty-four thousand cardholders, including men, women and children, and sponsored a smorgasbord of events and activities. Nevertheless, the Jackson District Library did start with a small group of forward-thinking individuals in the mid-1800s. Fortunately for today's generation, their efforts to "secure the greater good to the community" succeeded.[9]

10

Ella Sharp

Mother to Many

If you live in Jackson, you probably already know that Ella Merriman Sharp (1857–1912) had many claims to fame. The museum namesake was a civic leader, renowned philanthropist and supporter of women's rights, to name a few. But did you know this childless woman was a mother figure to many? A closer look at her life reveals that she was indeed a nurturing influence on youths, particularly young girls.

Throughout Ella's adult life, she devoted her time, energy and money to making the world a better place for future generations, thanks, in part, to the resources provided by her upper-middle-income parents. In 1881, Ella married businessman and attorney John Sharp, who also provided a comfortable life. In 1905, when Ella's last sibling died, she became the sole heir of her family's estate.

This accumulation of blessings added to her assets, but with whom would she share it? She and her husband had no children. Fortunately for posterity, Ella decided to invest much of her wherewithal in youth, becoming a mentor, advocate and financial backer for those in her sphere of influence. Receipts in the Ella Sharp Museum Archival Collections show she paid the tuition and room and board expenses for at least three women.

In addition, Ella took leadership roles in the Michigan State Federation of Women's Clubs during the 1880s, often serving on civic improvement committees that benefitted youth. She also initiated several local garden projects designed to beautify children's play and recreation areas.

Her efforts were not without resistance. In 1905, she wrote to the Cleveland Chamber of Commerce, asking if it would provide a speaker for a children's educational event. In reply, a chamber representative wrote, "It seems...a lecture to some of your older people would be more effective than one given simply to *children* [italics added]."

Undeterred, Ella continued to investigate progressive educational options for youth, drawing deeply from the well of knowledge, gathering concepts and inspirations near and far and then pouring them back on the community so that new ideas and improvements could sprout and blossom. A 1912 letter from the Kansas State Agricultural College responded to her interest in "movable schools" by sending her a brochure on the innovative program, which used wagons and trucks to bring modern agricultural tools and methods to rural areas.

That same year, the Michigan secretary of state appointed Ella as a delegate to the Child Welfare Conference of the National Congress of Mothers. The appointment was an ironic, yet appropriate, honor for a woman who was not a mother in the conventional sense of the word but who

Hillside Farm, part of the Ella Sharp Park and Museum, was bequeathed to the City of Jackson by Ella M. Sharp, a youth advocate and philanthropist. *Author's photo.*

had become a mother figure to many. The National Congress of Mothers, founded in 1897, focused on education, health and safety issues related to children and youth and evolved into what is now known as the National Parent Teachers Association.

When Ella died in 1912, she left her largest bequest, Hillside Farm, to the City of Jackson. Today, her gift is memorialized by the Ella Sharp Park and Ella Sharp Museum, a social, educational and recreational magnet for children of all ages. The gift encompasses 563 acres of a natural wonderland along the banks of the southwest branch of the Grand River. The park includes a golf course, flower gardens, hiking trails, basketball courts and soccer and softball fields, to name a few attractions.

It is a legacy that would have brought a smile to the face of a woman who may not have had children but whose generosity nevertheless created an extended family of grateful beneficiaries.[10]

Part II

JACKSON COUNTY TOWNSHIPS

II

Blackman Charter Township

Fun Facts

- The first settlers on land that is now part of Blackman Township were Lyman Pease in June 1830 and A.W. Daniels in September 1830.
- Blackman Township was part of Jacksonburg until 1857, when it was organized into a separate township.
- The name "Blackman" was chosen "to…honor the name of the first pioneer of the county," Jackson founder Horace Blackman.
- Historians characterized Blackman Township as being rich in minerals, including iron, coal and "large quarries of excellent limestone."
- Today, the township is known as the "Crossroads to Progress," the motto on township letterhead. Two major highways, I-94 and US 127, intersect in its boundaries providing an infrastructure that has benefitted many businesses and industries.[11]

From Everts & Stewart Combination Atlas Map of Jackson County, 1874.

UNDAUNTED COURAGE

The demands of frontier life required special qualities in the settlers who came here. Conventional rules simply didn't apply. Pioneers had to be tenacious, resourceful and willing to gamble on the unknown. Such were the characteristics of the Morrill family, who settled in Blackman Township seven years before Michigan became a state.

In the early fall of 1830, Edward Morrill, his friend Enoch Fifield and their families left an established life in New Hampshire for the promise of new opportunities in the untamed Michigan Territory. The prospective settlers traveled by boat through the Erie Canal to Detroit. Rather than splurge on horses and wagons for the eighty-mile trip from Detroit to what is now Jackson, these thrifty pioneers chose a cheaper mode of transportation: their feet. Undoubtedly, they also slept on the frosty ground en route.

On October 22, 1830, they planted their muddy boots on Jackson's turf for the first time, arriving at a log tavern in what would become Blackman Township. Finally, they could sleep with a roof over their heads. The tavern's floor, however, might not have been an improvement over the hard ground. According to local historians, the entire building—floor, walls, even the door—was composed of rounded logs or rails, similar to a stockade. If the group slept on the floor, which was likely, the experience would be like sleeping on concrete corduroy. As uncomfortable as that might have been, at least the group was protected from wolves that prowled throughout the night.

The pioneers hunkered down in the tavern throughout the winter of 1830–31. When the fresh green of spring emerged through the snowy blanket of winter, the two families combined their resources to buy land in what is today Blackman Township, with the Morrills taking the northern portion and the Fifields taking the southern portion of an eleven-acre patch. The men cleared their respective properties and built their homes.

In addition, Edward and Henry Morrill built and operated one of the first sawmills in this part of the state. The mill not only provided the lumber that built many of Jackson's early homes and businesses, but it also supplied the Michigan Central Railroad with ties and timbers during its construction through Jackson County.

Biographers were impressed with the Morrills' resourcefulness. One stated, "With undaunted courage they stepped into the heart of the primal wilderness, and, true lords of the heritage as they were, commanded the untamed conditions to stand ruled," adding that the family "subsisted on berries, wild game…and on fish taken from the Grand River."

Arthur Morrill, the third generation to live in Blackman Township, was born to Henry and Rachel Morrill in 1845. By now, the Village of Jackson was flourishing. The family's initial gamble in coming to this rough-hewn settlement had paid off, and their descendants were poised to reap the benefits. Sometime in adulthood, Arthur moved to the city of Jackson and formed a successful partnership, Morrill & Fuller Co., which provided carriage supplies. Arthur married Abbie Fifield, and the couple resided on Mechanic Street in the 1880s. He was listed as a hardware merchant, and based on his subsequent purchases, he must have been a successful one.

In 1893, the couple returned to their beloved Blackman Township and bought 77 acres in section 15. By 1895, they had expanded their holdings to 174 acres. This was an incredible jump for a family who originally came to Blackman Township on foot with next to nothing. One historian lauded the family, and the pioneer stock from which they came: "Nowhere…has there appeared…men and women more hardy, more resourceful, more tenacious of purpose." The privations endured by these pioneers may be little known in Jackson County today, but the fruit of their labors—a well-developed township—is apparent for all to see.[12]

NATIVE AMERICANS, PIONEERS AND MOBSTERS ALL STOPPED HERE

When some of the earliest Blackman Township settlers arrived in Jacksonburg in 1830, their first refuge was a log tavern that provided the weary pioneers with warmth, shelter and camaraderie. Amazingly, a structure on the same property, near what is now Lansing Avenue, still provides that service and much more.

The Roadhouse Grill and Bar at 4112 Lansing Avenue is known for its traditional hospitality with good food, good company and good drinks. But it also serves heaping helpings of history and scintillating side dishes of intrigue.

Co-owners Aleksander Denda and Leah Kalis-Denda say the Roadhouse is the spot where "American Indians, politicians, stagecoach drivers, bootleg runners, and possibly some ghosts" all had a seat at various points in history. As gathering places go, it may be among the oldest in Jackson County, sitting on land inhabited by Native Americans until the 1830s. In fact, the land across the street was once part of a Native American burial ground. Also nearby is the Fifield Cemetery, once owned by that family.

The presence of these cemeteries hints at the mysterious allure of the property, but there is so much more. A nearby trail, which has since evolved into Lansing Avenue, was a north–south route for stagecoaches and the site of a farewell feast for the last band of resident Native Americans in Jackson County. The July 6, 1924 *Jackson Citizen Patriot* reflected on the significance of the site: "[It] stands upon the exact spot where the departing feast of the last band of resident Indians of Jackson county was given.…The property at that time was owned and farmed by the Fifield family.…Mr. Fifield gave them a feast.…Afterwards members of the tribe…faced about and stood in silence, saluting the…man and his farm house with a farewell salute before leaving the section forever."

Over the years, the property passed through several hands, including owners who turned it into the Meadow Lark Inn, an eatery that sold home-cooked meals from homegrown poultry and produce. Later, it was transformed into a dining spot for banquets and possibly a mobster or two.

"Jackson was a kind of halfway stop between Chicago and Detroit, and we've heard from many old-time residents that the inn was a speakeasy for mobsters traveling that route," said Leah Kalis-Denda. Speakeasies were illicit liquor stores or night clubs during Prohibition (1920–33). Supposedly, imbibing patrons had to show a special card to get in.

The Dendas have also heard that a mobster who fell from grace may or may not be buried in a sand-filled portion of the basement. They speculate the rumor was started by racketeers who hid bootleg liquor in the spot and wanted to deter unwanted inspection. But who knows for sure? Perhaps some aspects of history are better left hidden.

By 1940, under new ownership, the Meadow Lark Inn had become a fine-dining restaurant specializing in surf and turf served on Blue Willow china with crystal goblets. In 1967, Albert and Justina Kalis bought the establishment and opened it as the Roadhouse Grill and Bar.

Is the Roadhouse Haunted?

Co-owners Aleksander Denda and Leah Kalis-Denda say longtime customers have raised the prospect of the building's haunting on several occasions. "People have heard strange music when there were no musicians playing. Others say they've felt pushed when no one was behind them. A psychic once told me there were so many voices vying for his attention, he had to leave," said Leah, chuckling. "It definitely adds to the mysterious allure of the place."

While the eatery survived Prohibition, its existence was threatened by a blaze that erupted on Memorial Day in 1970. According to reports, an intruder broke into the wooden building and set fire to boxes, causing about $55,000 worth of damage. Friends and family rallied to restore the building and were successful. The renovated Roadhouse Grill and Bar opened later that year, preserving as many original features as possible, including the wooden floor and glass-paned doors.

The Kalises' daughter, Leah, and her husband, Aleksander Denda, bought the bar in 2003 and have sought to preserve the historic feel, including taking off wall paneling to expose original hand-painted murals and creating solid, rustic wooden furniture. It's just the kind of atmosphere that would have made Blackman's pioneers feel right at home—perhaps a few ghosts too.[13]

12

Columbia Township

Fun Facts

- The first settlement was made by Reverend C.H. Swain in 1832. He also constructed the first sawmill and harvested the first wheat crop in 1833. Swain became the first postmaster at "Swainsville" in 1834. The town's name was changed to Brooklyn in 1836.
- Columbia Township, named by pioneer George Stranahan, was established in 1838 and set aside from Napoleon Township in 1839. At that time, the township had a population of 1,560 and included the settlements of Brooklyn, Clark's Lake and Jefferson.
- Lake Columbia, a pre-Depression project, was delayed until the winter of 1961–62, when over 840 acres of Columbia Township farmland were flooded along Goose Creek to form the private lake community that now encompasses about twelve miles of shoreline.
- Today, the Village of Brooklyn is a hub of activity during the summer because of the many lakes in a five-minute drive of the village and races at Michigan International Speedway, among other attractions.[14]

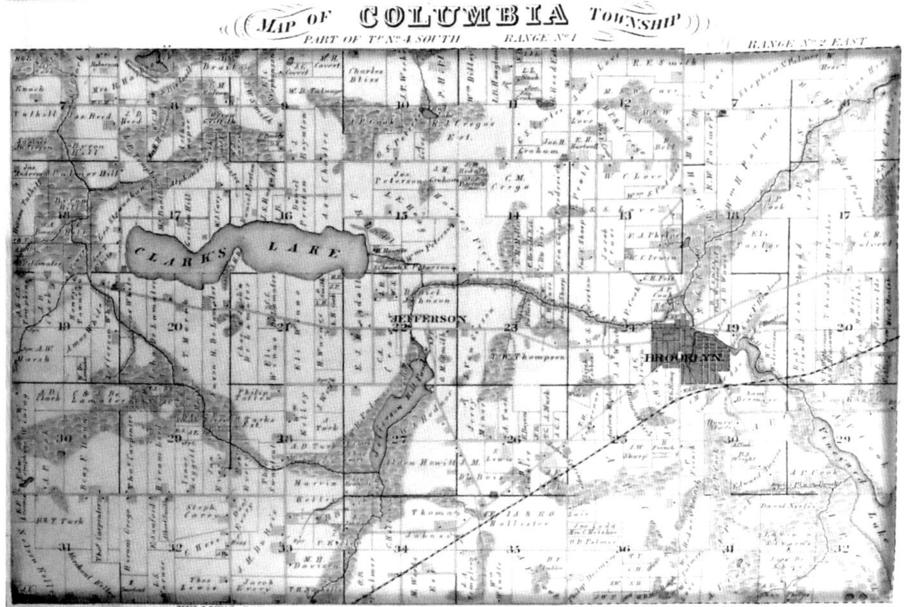

From Everts & Stewart Combination Atlas Map of Jackson County, 1874.

COLUMBIA'S PLUCKY PIONEER

Columbia residents owe their township's name and much more to George Stranahan (1783–1863), a public-spirited man known for his fearlessness and his green thumb—traits that served him well as one of the township's earliest settlers.

Stranahan, a New York native, first cast his eye on the Michigan Territory in the summer of 1833. He was beguiled by reports of abundant lakes and fertile soil. The wild beauty of the place appealed to his sense of adventure, so that summer, the explorer and his son-in-law, Leonard Taylor, traveled to Michigan to see for themselves.

Journeying through the untamed interior, Stranahan and Taylor arrived in Jackson County to behold "one of the most beautiful sheets of water in southern Michigan." They had come to Clark's Lake. (Early references are to "Clark's Lake," the postal reference is "Clarklake" and the community is commonly known as "Clark Lake.") The beauty of the shimmering water called to Stranahan like an enticing siren. It was love at first sight. The enamored New Yorker promptly bought four hundred acres on the north and west sides of the lake and then went home to tell his wife and seven children about the acquisition.

Shortly afterward, Stranahan returned to the lake property with his eldest son, George Jr., to take the pioneer version of a summer vacation. The duo cleared the land, built a log cabin and planted one hundred apple trees, establishing the first orchard in the township. By the next spring, the entire family was settled in their new home.

Their lake property likely had its charms, including sunsets that turned the water into glittering diamond fields, citrus aromas carried on autumn breezes and a pristine, unspoiled landscape. But it also had its drawbacks. The rustic accommodations may have been more primitive than Mrs. Stranahan expected. One night, she was awakened by plaintive squeals from the family's pig, which was kept in a nearby pen. She alerted George, who sprang from his bed, grabbed the nearest weapon he could find—a fire shovel—and headed out into the darkness. He was barely able to detect a predator attacking his pig, so he let down the fence for the pig to escape, only to open a pathway for a large, hairy beast that jumped on him.

The incident might have intimidated some, but it had the opposite effect on this fearless pioneer. Stranahan wielded his weapon with vengeance

Clark's Lake captivated George Stranahan, who bought four hundred acres on the north and west sides in 1833. *Courtesy Jackson District Library.*

and not only successfully defended himself but also saved the pig from being eaten alive by the wolf. Sadly, fate had other plans for the pig. Nine days later, the animal went mad from rabies and died. The wolf, however, was never a problem again.

While Stranahan was able to fend off predators, he was not able to divert illness, which frequently plagued his family. In 1840, his wife died, followed by his eldest daughter a few years later. In 1844, he remarried and lived for two more decades, making many contributions to Columbia Township. Biographers described Stranahan as a "public spirited man." He served as justice of the peace and road commissioner, among other offices.

In addition, Stranahan provided land for the first Clark Lake School on the southern edge of his property and had the honor of naming the township after his native county in New York. Columbia's fearless pioneer was laid to rest in Clarklake Cemetery in 1864. His accomplishments may be little known today, but the township still bears the name he chose.[15]

BIG BANDS AND A BEACH BAR

While the potential of Clark Lake's east side remained hidden to most in the 1920s, it was tantalizingly evident to entrepreneur Leo Steinem. When Steinem, father of renowned feminist Gloria Steinem, gazed at the sparkling water, he saw more than placid waves lapping the shoreline. He envisioned an enchanted pavilion where hundreds of patrons danced under the stars to the hottest bands in the land—all wrapped in an aura of magic.

So, Steinem, a frequent vacationer from Toledo, bought thirty acres on the east end and built a 99-foot-wide by 130-foot-long dance pavilion at the end of a 100-foot dock that projected out over the shallows. The open-air pavilion, named Ocean Beach Pier, could accommodate up to 1,200 couples seeking a chance to "dance under the stars and over the water." A dance floor covered with polished black and white terrazzo added to the allure. The entire structure rested on white oak piling garlanded with colored lights. To provide a premium recreation area fit for the first-rate attraction, Steinem trucked in tons of white sand, creating an enticing swimming beach around the structure.

Ocean Beach Pier opened with great fanfare on Memorial Day in 1928 and was an immediate hit, drawing fans throughout Michigan and Ohio. It also attracted such nationally known entertainers as Guy Lombardo,

Ocean Beach Pier was a dancing and entertainment hot spot on the east side of Clark's Lake in the early 1900s. *Courtesy John Collins.*

Duke Ellington and Count Basie. It was, as Steinem hoped, the hottest of hot spots.

The pavilion flourished for fifteen years, but in the early 1940s, business began to falter due to the effects of World War II and gas rationing. Rather than watch his beloved creation slowly deteriorate, Steinem had the structure demolished sometime in 1944. But the magic lingered in the memories of many, including Harry Collins, who had worked there as a restaurant manager. Collins bought the property from Steinem in 1946 and built a bar and restaurant across the road from where the pavilion once jutted out over the water.

The Beach Bar opened on July 27, 1946, specializing in hamburgers, French fries and fried fish. Collins and his wife, Marie (whom he met at Ocean Beach Pier), operated the establishment with great success throughout the '40s and '50s. By 1959, they were ready to retire. Since none of their children wanted to take over the establishment at that time, they sold the business to Bob and Anna Gage.

In 1976, their son Tom Collins and his wife, Peggy, had a change of heart and purchased the establishment, expanding and remodeling it.

Peggy introduced fresh sandwiches and homemade soups. Tom filled the building with memorabilia from the first water ski on the lake to the original tables and chairs from Ocean Beach Pier. Customers loved it, and business boomed.

Today, the Beach Bar, the oldest public establishment on the lake, is owned by Tom and Peggy's son, John Collins. He has added to the menu and expanded the building. And while the pavilion is long gone, the magic from almost a century ago remains.[16]

13

Concord Township

Fun Facts

- The first settler in what is now Concord Township was John Acker, who built a log cabin there in 1831.
- Before 1837, Concord Township was part of Spring Arbor. When it was first set off into a distinct township, it encompassed territory that included Pulaski Township. In 1837, Pulaski was made a separate town and the present limits of Concord Township were established.
- The township was named by pioneer Thomas McGee because he said it was a place where neighbors and friends "lived together in peace and harmony."
- The first school was opened in 1835 with teacher Mary McGee.
- At least three Concord residents participated in the Underground Railroad during the early to mid-1800s: Thomas McGee, David Smalley and James Taylor.
- In 1906, Buffalo Bill Cody came to the village with his well-known show featuring wild animals, trick performances, theatrical reenactments and fancy shooting. The show was set up in an open field behind the Universalist church on Union Street.
- The township is known as a well-watered, fertile agricultural region, producing crops of all kinds.[17]

From Everts & Stewart Combination Atlas Map of Jackson County, 1874.

NEW HORIZONS

Some historians say Mary Ida Mann and Jessie Ellen Mann, namesakes of Concord's Mann House, were freethinkers eager to break social, educational and occupational barriers. Others say the sisters were products of their era, benefitting from nineteenth-century middle-class parents who wanted to educate their daughters when schools were expanding. Regardless of which characterization is more fitting, one thing is certain: these sisters were unafraid to explore new horizons.

Thankfully, both also wanted to share their legacy with the public, bequeathing their charming Victorian house to the people of Michigan. Their gift, the Mann House on Hanover Street, is filled with original furnishings, mementos from their travels and late nineteenth-century heirlooms that provide a snapshot of family life in the 1880s. The museum also offers fascinating insights into the self-sufficient, forward-thinking women who lived there.

The bright yellow-and-green trimmed house was built by Daniel Sears Mann and Ellen Keeler Mann in the winter of 1883–84. The couple and their young daughters, Mary Ida and Jessie, moved from their farm two miles west of the village into the residence in March 1884. Their third daughter, Elizabeth, died as an infant around 1882. Some historians speculate that Elizabeth's death prompted the move into the heart of the village, bringing the family closer to medical assistance, community life and schools.

Both Daniel and Ellen valued education. When Ellen graduated from Michigan Normal School (now Eastern Michigan University) in 1871,

Sisters Mary Ida and Jessie Ellen Mann bequeathed their house to the State of Michigan. Today, the Mann House museum is a popular tourist destination. *Author's photo.*

less than 1 percent of American women between the ages of eighteen and twenty-one attended an institution of higher learning. As an example of just how radical Ellen's course of action was, two years after she graduated, Dr. Edward Clark, an American physician and author, characterized coeducation as dangerous and ill-advised in his book *Sex in Education; Or, A Fair Chance for the Girls.*

Undaunted by this and other criticisms, Ellen not only embraced education, but she also promoted it. She taught for one year in Parma before marrying Daniel, who attended Hillsdale and Olivet Colleges, in 1873. He obviously shared his wife's radical sentiments, because both parents encouraged daughters Mary Ida and Jessie to excel in everything they did. Books kept by the family bear a silent witness to the breadth of literature made available to the girls, from *Macbeth* by William Shakespeare to *Uncle Tom's Cabin* by Harriet Beecher Stowe.

As the girls matured, the house became a social center of the town. One can almost imagine the sight of carriages coming and going from the popular spot, the sound of greetings at the door and the lively conversations in the parlor. Historians believe the girls looked up to their mother as a role model and gladly followed in her footsteps. Mary Ida graduated from Michigan State Normal School, focusing on physical education for women. She taught at the University of Missouri and the University of Chicago, among other institutions. Jessie also attended Michigan State Normal School and taught for several years in smaller districts, including Parma and Concord.

Jessie then returned to school at the University of Michigan and graduated with a bachelor's degree in mathematics in 1906. To put this accomplishment into perspective, in 1900, only 10 percent of the United States population had a high school diploma. Jessie and Mary Ida, on the other hand, both had college degrees.

The Mann sisters went on to travel the world and continued to break social and occupational barriers. Jessie taught mathematics for Battle Creek Public Schools for twenty years, and Mary Ida went to the Philippines as a teacher, where she married Charles Cady. Mary Ida moved to various locations in the United States with her husband but returned to her childhood home in 1942, after her husband died. Neither sister had children.

Mary Ida Cady died in 1959, and Jessie Mann lived in the house until she died in 1969. They are buried at Maple Grove Cemetery, Concord, with their parents and grandparents. As a tribute to the town they loved, their wills bequeathed their house to the State of Michigan. In 1970, the house was named a Michigan State Historic Site and was listed on the

National Register of Historic Places. The museum, arranged as if the sisters had just stepped out for a moment, is operated by the Michigan History Center, Michigan Department of Natural Resources and is a favorite tour destination.

Visitors who look closely will sense an independent, forward-thinking spirit in the library of a family who valued education and in the mementos of young women unafraid to explore new horizons.[18]

THE REIGN OF TERROR

The Village of Concord was known for many things in 1917: bountiful harvests, plentiful timber and neighbors who lived in harmony and, well, concord.

Such peaceful ambience was rocked to its core one November morning in 1917, when an armed robbery took place in the very heart of the friendly little village. The daring heist, at Farmer's State Bank, involved gunfire, a series of explosions and the theft of $18,200, making it one of Jackson County's biggest robberies to that point. Long-forgotten newspaper reports give further details of the "reign of terror" this incident inflicted on the quiet village. Around 1:30 a.m. on November 9, a gang of heavily armed bandits drove into town and began systematically isolating the village. Two men went to Concord's Michigan Central ticket and telegraph office, cut telegraph wires and held a frightened ticket agent at gunpoint.

After severing all communication in the village, gang members proceeded to the bank. One stood outside as guard while others battered down the bank's front door. They then ignited a series of explosions that blew open the vault, shattered windows and demolished furniture, sending glass shards and wood splinters flying through the air like buckshot. The repercussions were heard miles away.

When bank vice president Frank Aldrich, who lived next door to the bank, looked out his window, he saw a damaged building emerge from the smoke, with paper money swirling in the air like autumn leaves. Concerned citizens ran helter-skelter in what amounted to comedy and tragedy at the same time.

One resident attempted to sound a fire alarm and was fired on twice, with bullets missing him both times. Another citizen raced to the scene wielding a gun, only to have the tables turned by a bandit who ordered him to "beat it damn quick, or I'll blow your brains out!"

CITIZEN PRESS

LAST EDITION

FRIDAY, NOVEMBER 9, 1917. PRICE: PER COPY, TWO CENTS. A WEEK, TEN CENTS. 24 PAGES

HIS CABINET IS JAILED

LANSING GAS CO. IS DENIED A FRANCHISE

Lansing, Mich., Nov. 9.—Lansing denied the Lansing Fuel and Gas Company a fifteen-year extension of its franchise yesterday in a special election, giving a majority for the extension but not the necessary three-fifths. The vote was 1,671 for and 1,248 against, a defeat of 81 votes. The extension was asked that the company might float bonds for improvements and extensions.

Russ Bonds Slump in Wall Street.

New York, Nov. 9.—Russian government bonds which are dealt in on the curb reflected the lower exchange rates today. The 6 1-2's sold at 54 and the 5 1-2's at 45, representing further depreciations of four and three per cent respectively, to new low records.

RUSS UPHEAVAL CREATES ALARM AT WASHINGTON

Interest in the Startling De-

CONCORD BANK VAULT IS 'BLOWN' BY BANDITS WHO ESCAPE WITH $18,200 CASH

CANUCKS AWAIT HUN ATTACK ON PASSCHENDAELE

Believed Hindenberg will Order Troops to Regain the Village at All Costs.

Outlaw Band Terrorizes the Peaceful Little Village in the Dead of Night.

CITIZEN IS FIRED UPON

Yeggs Cut Wires, Meanwhile Covering M. C. Telegraph Operator With Guns.

(Staff Special to The Citizen Press.)

Concord, Mich., Nov. 9.—After cutting all wire communications leading out of the town, a band of professional bank robbers blew the doors off the safe at the Farmers' State bank here early this morning.

JACKSON BOYS AT CAMP CUSTER IN BIG REVIEW

Twenty Thousand Men Pass Before Gen. Dickman in First Grand Parade.

Outlaws terrorized the Village of Concord during a brazen bank robbery in 1917. *Taken from* Jackson Citizen Patriot *microfilm at the Jackson District Library.*

A few minutes later, the thieves scrambled out of the bank with their loot and leaped into a waiting car that took off in a southerly direction. Soon after, another car returned to the village and took an easterly route. The quiet Village of Concord was turned upside down in the aftermath.

The confusion continued when Calhoun County sheriff's officers suspected a car heading west of Parma was one of the getaway cars and flagged for the driver to stop. The innocent motorist, fearing that a stick-up was unfolding, put the pedal to the metal and roared past. This confirmed the suspicions of the officers, who opened fire with a vengeance. Their action, in turn, confirmed the suspicions of the motorist, who sped up even faster, adding to the tragicomedy.

When the dust settled, authorities determined the motorist was a law-abiding citizen who happened to be at the wrong place at the wrong time. And while the driver may have been unlucky in his choice of location, he was uncannily fortunate otherwise—none of the twenty-nine bullets that penetrated his car injured him.

This historic building in Concord housed the township's first bank in 1884. *Author's photo.*

News articles reporting on any trials or verdicts involving the heist have not been discovered, suggesting the robbers were never caught. It would appear that the bandits got the upper hand, since their identities were never determined, and the stolen loot was never recovered. But that's not the end of the story.

The bank building that they stormed stands, to this day, at the southeast corner of Main and Hanover Streets in Concord—a monument to the perseverance of Concord's residents who, posterity will prove, had the last word in this drama. The building, which housed the First National Bank of Concord in 1884, Farmers State Bank in 1886 and a succession of other banks due to mergers and reorganizations, was recently purchased and renovated by a local businessman, who had the exterior painted with murals reflecting his interest in cars and history. And while the robbers are long gone, the historic structure remains as an object of enduring admiration.[19]

14

Grass Lake Charter Township

Fun Facts

- Grass Lake became a township in 1832 and comprised the county east of the meridian. Its current boundaries were established in 1836.
- In 1829 or 1830, David Sterling squatted on land south of the present village and built a log cabin. He was later joined by George C. Pease, Daniel Thayer, John Ritchie and Ralph Updike, among other early settlers.
- In 1831, settler Daniel Walker was appointed the first postmaster. He also opened the first school. Updike built the first sawmill, and Sterling opened the first tavern.
- In 1842, the Michigan Central Railroad was completed through Jackson, and the depot was located about where the present village now stands.
- Tradition holds that the township was named after the "beautiful sheet of water" now known as Grass Lake, as well as the "luxuriant wild grass" that caught pioneers' attention.[20]

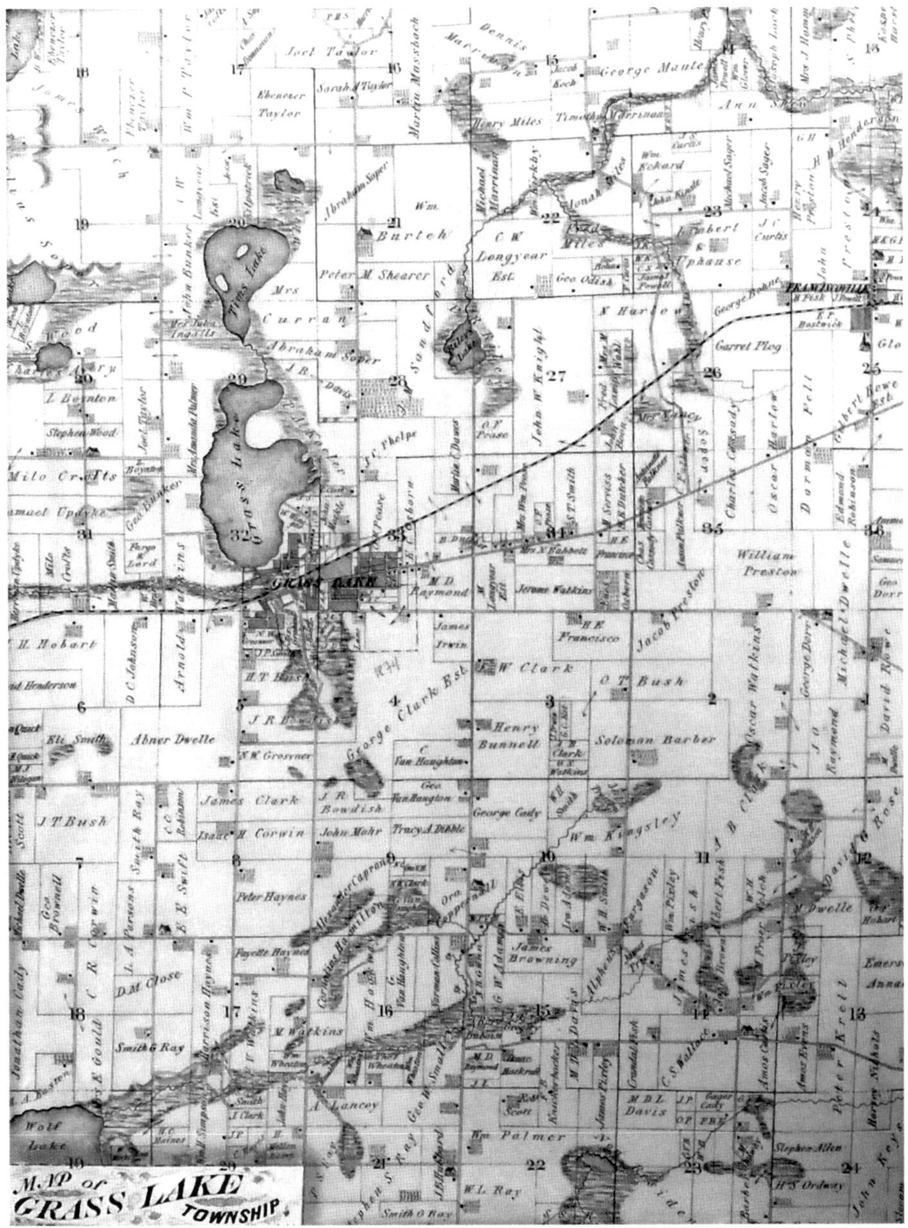

From Everts & Stewart Combination Atlas Map of Jackson County, 1874.

A Blaze of Glory

One of Jackson County's greatest resorts went up and came down in a blaze of glory in the early 1900s, leaving only fantastic tales, picturesque postcards and an invisible but haunting presence that lingers in lake lore.

The resort was the brainchild of William A. Boland (1848–1918), a wealthy New Englander who had fond memories of his family's farm at Grass Lake. Boland, an entrepreneur and investor, dreamed of a development that would give him a reason to return to his beloved childhood home, attract others to its midst and produce a profit in the process. The apple of his eye was Big Wolf Lake in southern Grass Lake Township.

To pursue his dreams, Boland leased thirty acres of lake property from an area developer and spent $20,000 constructing Wolf Lake Casino, an elaborate three-story structure built over the water. An August 22, 1902 newspaper article painted an extravagant picture of the development. Descriptions detailed a 62-by-130-foot dance hall on the third floor, a roof garden and a "first-class restaurant" headed by a famous chef who specialized in fish, frog legs and fried chicken.

To facilitate access to the resort, Boland built an interurban electric railway that transported guests to and from the remote spot. Trains ran from early in the morning until the wee hours, which was a good thing because during the dedication, the Boos Band entertained guests until 1:30 a.m. Trains left Jackson every thirty minutes, and more than ten thousand people rode them to and from the casino in 1904 alone.

Boland also opened another form of access to his tourist magnet: dock privileges. A 1902 article stated, "The Boland people wish it understood that the dock privileges at the casino are free to all, and that owners of steamboats, launches, sail and rowboats, can have use of the docks without any expense whatever."

By all accounts, Wolf Lake Casino was a raving success. A May 1903 ball held at the resort by the Street Railway Employees Union featured dinner and dancing in rooms decorated with streamers of red, white and blue bunting. Guests also could stroll along a roof garden overflowing with palms and flowering plants. An article about the ball stated, "The night was decidedly chilly, the lake being wind-swept, but within the glass-enclosed dancing hall, all was light, cheerfulness and happiness."

All was not cheerfulness and happiness at the casino the early morning of September 19, 1913, though. Around 3:00 a.m., a fire started in the kitchen, spread throughout the grandiose structure, lit the sky like a funeral pyre

Wolf Lake Casino in Grass Lake Township was a premier resort in the early 1900s. It was destroyed by fire in 1913. *Courtesy Jackson District Library.*

and left nothing "but a few charred and burned-off posts arising from the waters." According to news reports, the fire started in the stove, which was used "up to a late hour." It progressed rapidly, consuming the casino, eight launches and a nearby cottage.

A witness said the grass had been very dry and the wild blaze "sent embers all around." Other eyewitnesses said rain later in the early morning wet the grass in the nick of time, preventing the fire from spreading to all the cottages on that side of the lake. The article concluded, "Not a trace of the superstructure is left and most of the foundation is burned to the water's level."

In the aftermath, Boland decided it was time to return to what mattered most. He retired from business and spent the rest of his years on his family's homestead after repurchasing the farm. In 1918, he died on the same property where he was born. His obituary said, "Few Jackson County men enjoyed a wider acquaintance throughout the United States…and few men took a more active part in…business development…than did he." William Anson Boland was buried at Grass Lake West Cemetery, but the legend of his Wolf Lake Casino lives on.[21]

CROSSED PATHS

Isaac Whisple (1843–1906) fought for the Union army and wore blue. George Daft (1839–1912) fought for the Confederate army and wore gray. Regardless of their differing allegiances, the Civil War soldiers had one thing in common: Grass Lake Township.

Northerner Isaac was born in 1843, the son of German immigrants Peter and Rebeca Whisple. The Whisples were among the earliest pioneers of Grass Lake, settling in the township about 1836. Isaac, who received a common-school education, was "reared in the farming pursuits" and remained on the homestead until 1860, when he married Melissa Wright. Two years later, on July 30, 1862 (about one year after the Civil War began), he enlisted in Company C, Michigan Eighth Infantry Regiment.

Southerner George was born in Virginia in 1839. He was the second of fifteen children born to Jacob and Margaret Daft. He enlisted as a private in Company F, Thirty-First Virginia Infantry Regiment on May 24, 1861. Throughout the war, his regiment reported heavy casualties, from Second Manassas to Gettysburg.

While George's Confederate service revolved around Virginia, Isaac's Union contingent was known as the wandering regiment because it was always on the move, beginning with General Sherman's South Carolina offensive to establish a navy blockade. From there, it marched to Virginia, increasing the possibility that the men's paths crossed from opposite sides of the firing line.

Did the bullets from their guns cross paths, whizzing by the other's head? We will never know, of course. It is known, however, that Isaac was captured by Confederate soldiers at Watertown, Virginia, and was transported to Libby Prison in Richmond, Virginia, where he spent three months in a facility known for its mistreatment of prisoners and high mortality rate.

Likewise, George was captured by Union soldiers and spent several miserable months at Camp Chase Military Prison in Columbus, Ohio. He was captured and incarcerated a second time at an undisclosed location. In this sense, both men would have shared a bond of sad fellowship as captives who likely experienced hunger, deprivation and abuse on either side of the line. Fortunately, both also were survivors.

Isaac was released, perhaps through a prisoner exchange. At the expiration of his term of enlistment, he was mustered out with his regiment in the fall of 1865 and returned to Grass Lake. He is listed in the 1870 and 1890 U.S. censuses as a "farmer in Grass Lake" and the father of two children.

George was ultimately paroled at Charleston, West Virginia, where he rejoined his family. In 1871, he married Pauline Lake. The couple had two children born in the South. Around 1880, George and his immediate family moved to Michigan. George is listed in the U.S. census of that year as a "farmer" in nearby Lenawee County, meaning that he was a virtual neighbor of Isaac. Their common occupation as farmers and their proximity suggest that, once again, the paths of these two veterans might have crossed.

What brought this Son of the South so far into former Northern territory? Perhaps a South ravaged by war could no longer feed the Daft family. Or perhaps some relatives had already moved north? For whatever reason, this Confederate veteran found his way to the Great Lakes State, where two Daft children were born on northern soil.

George died in Lenawee County on February 1, 1912, and was buried at Grass Lake, where his son Stewart Daft resided. Isaac Whisple died on September 5, 1906, and was buried at the Fulton Street Cemetery, Grand Rapids, where he had recently moved. But from 1880 to about 1900, both men lived as neighbors and both worked as farmers.

The Daft family's choice of final resting place for George gives the Grass Lake East Cemetery, well into Union territory, the unique distinction of

The gravesite of George E. Daft is the only Confederate grave in Jackson County, according to local historians. *Author's photo, Grass Lake East Cemetery.*

being the only cemetery in Jackson County to inter a Confederate veteran. Scott Gerych, curator for the Michigan Military Heritage Museum, Grass Lake, and Ethan Smith, founder of the Historical Campaign, a nonprofit educational organization specializing in the Civil War, are unaware of any other Confederate grave in Jackson County. Gerych hopes Daft's grave will inspire people to research the reasons for this complicated war. Certainly, the crossed paths of these soldiers show they had much in common, including their little-known connection to Grass Lake.[22]

15
Hanover Township

Fun Facts

- Hanover was originally part of Spring Arbor Township. It was established as a separate township in 1836.
- The first settler in the township was Abiel Tripp, who came from Rutland, Vermont, in the spring of 1832. Salmon Hale, his stepson, came with him and plowed the first land broken in the town.
- The first flouring mill was built by George A. Baldwin around 1842. It prompted what was known as the Village of Baldwin, but the Ft. Wayne, Saginaw & Jackson Railroad later changed the name to Horton.
- The first post office was established in section 21 in 1836, with John Crittenden as postmaster.
- Hanover was historically noted for its "enterprising and prosperous farmers."[23]

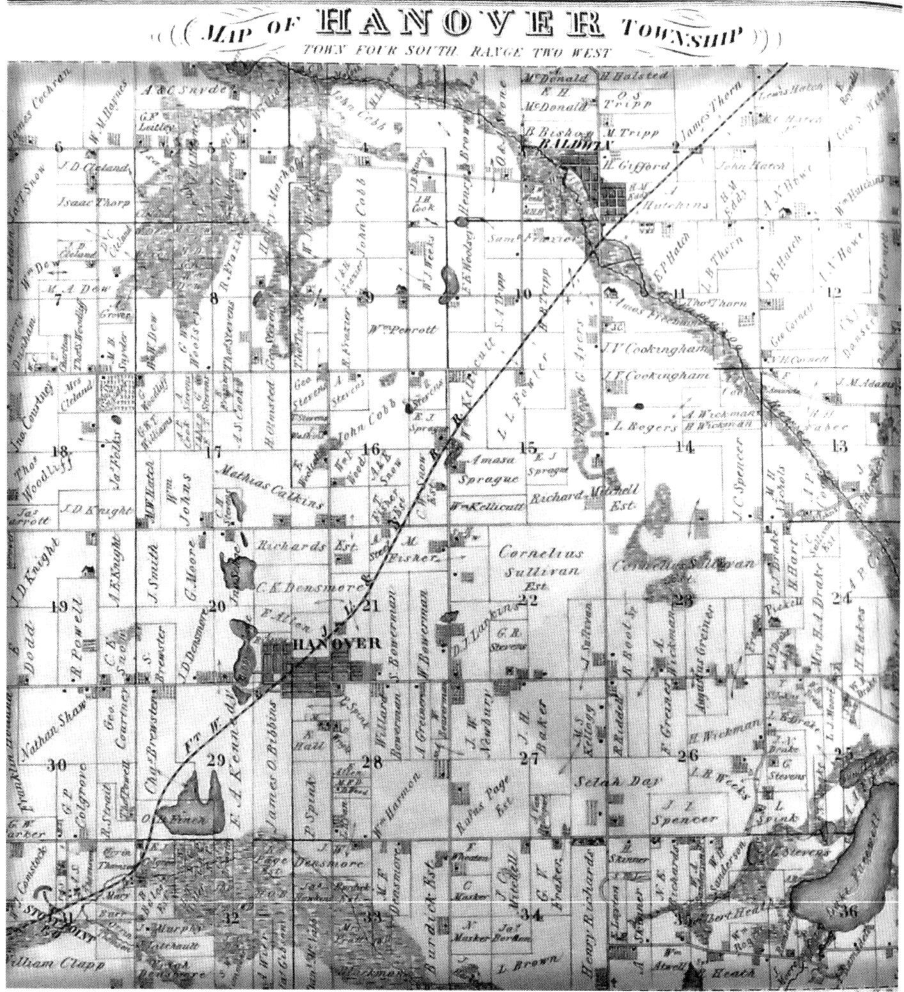

From Everts & Stewart Combination Atlas Map of Jackson County, 1874.

Blossom Like a Rose

History isn't always found in headlines. Sometimes, it's found in the quiet determination of unsung heroes who improved their surroundings despite obstacles—pioneers who used their strength and abilities to make rough places blossom without recognition or fanfare. This was the case with the Densmores of Hanover, a humble Quaker family who contributed to the growth and development of the community in their own quiet ways.

Abiel Densmore (1787–1852), of Scottish descent, married Abigail Kelley (1794–1876), of Irish descent, in 1814. The couple from Maine had five sons and five daughters. Biographers say the family had "exemplary habits, using neither liquor nor tobacco" and were highly respected for their integrity.

In 1839, the Densmores moved to Michigan, settling in Hanover, which was then a fledgling township only three years old. Considering Abiel's occupation as a farmer, they must have greeted the rolling green countryside of Hanover, originally known as Oak Openings, with optimism.

Family members also must have been resilient. Summing their challenges, one historian wrote, "The pioneers of Hanover endured great privations and suffered much from fever and ague, or chill-fever, which was almost sure to find its way into every house. In addition to this, there was a scarcity of provisions; consequently, they had to go…40 to 50 miles to mill, and sometimes wait a day or two for their turns to get grinding."

That hardship was turned to joy in 1842, when George A. Baldwin built the first flouring mill in Hanover near a stream. Moving water was needed to flow onto water wheels that turned a series of gears and stones that ultimately ground grain into four. Thanks to Baldwin's undertaking, the Densmores finally had a mill in their township—an essential amenity since bread was a staple of pioneers' diets.

Still, pioneer life took its toll. In 1852, family patriarch Abiel died and was buried at Hanover Cemetery. His widow would live for twenty-four more years and see more changes in the village she now called home, including the confusion in 1870 when the Ft. Wayne, Saginaw & Jackson Railroad finished building tracks through the town. The railroad, in its wisdom, decided to change the existing village name from "Baldwin" to "Horton," although "Baldwin" still lingers in township lore.

That same year, life might have gotten a little easier for the family when the first grocery store was established. Up to that point, pioneer families were responsible for producing their own goods or traveling long distances to buy supplies in larger cities. If Hanover's store was like most, it greeted customers with a potpourri of scents, including ripe cheese, pickles, cured meats, tobacco, kerosene and feed. Generally, such stores were dimly lit, lined on every wall by shelving and filled to the brim with boxes, barrels and crates.

As a shopper in the Midwest during the mid-1800s, Abigail could expect to pay about sixteen cents for a dozen eggs or pound of butter, eighteen cents for a bushel of potatoes and twelve cents per pound for ham. In the winter, when cast-iron stoves were burning coal or wood for heat, she likely found a thin layer of soot covering items.

JACKSON COUNTY

John W. Densmore
BORN, SIDNEY, ME, NOV. 2ND 1816.

THE DENSMORE BROTHERS.

Abiel Densmore, the father of the gentlemen whose faces appear on this
page, was born in Sydney, Maine, February 8, 1787. The mother, Abigail
Densmore, was born at Cape Cod, Mass., April 13, 1794, and was married
to Mr. Densmore in 1814. They settled in the town of Sydney, Maine, and
it was here that their large family of children were born.
John W. Densmore, the eldest, was born October 2, 1816; Charles K.
Densmore, January 21, 1827; Uriah H. and Josiah F. Densmore, April 8,
1828; Joshua D. Densmore, July 31, 1831; Moses F. Densmore, July 7, 1834.
Aside from these there were five sisters, four of whom are now living in this
state, and a brother who died some years since. In 1839 the family moved to
Michigan and settled in Hanover, where the father died September 10, 1852.
The children have all grown up and married and the sons are all settled on
farms in Hanover near each other. Mrs. Densmore is able to number as
her own, aside from the ten children who still live, fifty-one grandchildren
and thirty-three great-grandchildren, or in all ninety-four now living.
The parents and eldest son were members of the Society of Friends, the
other children belong to the Methodist Church. The brothers are upright.
honorable men, highly respected by the whole
their worth and integrity.

John Densmore and his family were among Quaker pioneers in Hanover Township. *From Everts & Stewart Combination Atlas Map of Jackson County, 1874.*

Another important building was established in 1874, when Abigail's Quaker community constructed its own house of worship at a cost of $1,600. Although the other Densmore children became Methodists later in life, Abigail and her oldest son, John W. Densmore, continued to practice the Quaker faith, known for its rejection of elaborate religious ceremonies, lack of official clergy and belief in spiritual equality for men and women.

In 1876, Abigail died and was buried beside her husband at Hanover Cemetery. She and her husband never sought the spotlight or made the headlines, but they were among unsung heroes who contributed to the township's development in countless anonymous ways. Before Abigail and her husband died, they probably looked back on their lives with the kind of gratification best summed by *History of Jackson County, Michigan*, published by Inter-State Publishing Co., "The pioneers of Hanover have the satisfaction of knowing that they have acted in a very important part in the great role of Western civilization—that they have been instrumental in making rough places smooth and desert places to blossom as a rose."[24]

Touchable History

Eva Greiner Moses (1897–1979) and her family loved music. The talented Hanover residents often traveled around the area playing various instruments at dances. Had the Greiners known how much their love of music would inspire Lee Conklin (1895–1989), a friend of Eva's, they might have been amused. But that outcome had yet to transpire when Eva gave Conklin his first reed organ in 1965.

This reed organ in the Lee Conklin Antique Reed Organ and History Museum, Hanover, was the first specimen collected by the museum's namesake. *Author's photo.*

Unlike pipe organs, reed organs generate sound as air flows past a vibrating piece of metal called a reed. Reed organs, lighter and more portable than pipe organs, were commonly used in smaller churches and private homes in the nineteenth century.

Eva's gift, made by Mason & Hamlin Organ Co. in 1884, was a sign of things to come. Conklin, a farmer and woodworker near Hanover, was captivated by the airy, accordion-like sounds it produced, so he began collecting reed organs in his barn. Although he never learned to play them, he often used his woodworking tools to fix or replace missing parts. He particularly enjoyed the visits of Frances Hartmann, a Hanover music teacher who played tunes for him.

One thing led to another, and as Conklin's extensive collection grew, he began looking for a way to share their beauty and charm with others. That prompted the founding of the Hanover–Horton Area Historical Society in

1977. The society leased and then purchased the Hanover School at 105 Fairview Street to display Conklin's expanding collection. The resulting Lee Conklin Antique Reed Organ and History Museum opened on December 18, 1977.

The museum sits on the property where the original two-story brick schoolhouse stood in 1874. The Georgian Revival–style school has its own interesting story, serving the community until 1910, when the original building was destroyed by fire. Residents rallied to bring new life from the ashes, salvaging the scorched bricks and using them to build a similar foundation and floorplan. The rebuilt school opened in 1911 and held classes until 1958. By 1977, the old building was falling apart, and the historical society stepped in to restore the structure and establish its museum in the former school that same year.

Conklin lived long enough to see his beloved collection displayed in a museum that attracts admirers from around the world. Many visitors want to not only see the antiques but also play them. In this sense, the museum contains a touchable, audible history that has become a hands-on experience.

Lee Conklin died on May 22, 1989, and was buried at Sunset View Cemetery, Hillsdale. Today, the museum houses more than one hundred

The Lee Conklin Antique Reed Organ and History Museum, Hanover, is listed on the National Register of Historic Places. *Author's photo.*

working antique reed organs displayed in the school's former gym. The collection includes parlor, cottage and church organs, along with elegant rosewood melodeons. The oldest date that can be verified is 1856. The smallest specimen is the size of an accordion, but there are huge models as well as frilly ones, self-playing reed organs and much more—all from different time periods. In addition, five classrooms in the museum showcase local history. It is a remarkable legacy for a man inspired by a simple gift. The music of Lee Conklin lives on.[25]

16
Henrietta Township

Fun Facts

- Henrietta Township was among the earliest trading places in central Michigan. A French fur trader known by various names, including John Batteese Berrard, settled here in 1816. Batteese Lake was named after him. A historical plaque commemorating these milestones stands near Bunkerhill Road.
- In the early 1830s, John and Robert Davison settled in the area and built the first sawmill. Also that year, John Westren bought 1,800 acres of land around Pleasant Lake and divided it into farms. Early settlers on the land included Hiram Archer, Thomas Tanner, Alfred Hall, Sherlock Patrick, James Suylant, Abram Bunker and E. Doggett.
- The township was organized in 1837, with the name West Portage. It is likely a reference to tributaries of the Portage River, which runs along the township's southern boundary. In 1839, the name was changed to Henrietta by Henry Hurd, Esq., in honor of his native home in New York.
- The first post office opened in 1838, and John Davidson served as the first postmaster.[26]

From Everts & Stewart Combination Atlas Map of Jackson County, 1874.

THE LAST FRENCH TRAPPER

One of Henrietta Township's most celebrated pioneers, the one who inspired a lake name and a historical marker, is a man of mystery. His French surname has been transliterated several different ways, all with a common thread. Historians say he lived in what is now Henrietta Township and traded with Native Americans for at least twenty-one years before Michigan became a state. His life is the stuff legend—a Jacksonian Paul Bunyon. But who was he?

A plaque near Bunkerhill Road on the east side of Batteese Lake sheds some light on the mystery man. It states, "This boulder marks the site where John Batteese Berrard built the first Indian trading post in Jackson County." A grave marker installed by the Daughters of the American Revolution in Nims Cemetery further identifies him as "John B. Berrard" (1790–1855).

Early historians have filled in a few more blanks. *The History of Jackson County, Michigan*, published in 1881, referred to Henrietta's first settler as "John Baptiste Barboux, an Indian trader," who arrived around 1816. Another historian referred to Henrietta's first settler as "John Baptiste Barboreau," a Frenchman who settled here in 1816 and traded with Indians. Related surnames include Battise, Batteese and Boreaux. Clearly, English-speaking historians didn't know what to do with his French name, but the descriptions are similar enough that there's no doubt it is the same man.

Fortunately, archival records have fleshed out his character a bit more, beginning with a Canadian birth certificate showing that "Jean Baptiste Berard" was born in 1790 in Quebec. Historians say he came to what is now Henrietta Township in 1816. Apparently, he liked what he saw enough to remain as a squatter. On July 10, 1832, a "Jean B. Berard" filed a claim in the Detroit land office for property in the Michigan-Toledo strip, which included Jackson. The 1840 U.S. census confirms that "John Bonard/Barrard" resided in Henrietta Township.

In piecing together archival evidence with historical accounts, a clearer picture of this enigmatic pioneer emerges from the shadows. It is a picture of a French Canadian voyageur, trapper and fur trader who migrated to the undeveloped interior of Michigan from Canada around 1816. As a fur trader, he would have been attracted to the Great Lakes and Michigan's inland waterways—an economic lifeline for trappers, farmers and lumbermen. On these waters, fur traders set their traps, and flatboats traveled to and fro, carrying crops, logs and pelts.

Berard's travels through Michigan came to a stop when he stepped foot in Henrietta Township. The lush landscape and streams appealed to him

Jean Baptiste Berard was a French trapper and fur trader who lived in Henrietta Township. *From Inter-State Publishing, History of Jackson County, Michigan, 1881.*

immediately. The wanderer decided to settle down on the east shore of the lake that would bear his name. Berard established a thriving business, which historians describe as "the earliest trading place in central Michigan." The business was housed in a log cabin "in which he kept a large stock of goods to swap with the Indians for furs." In fact, some said he "had more goods than there were in Jackson." Descriptions of his dwelling conjure visions of a rustic cabin nestled under pines, smelling of tanned hides and furs and filled to the brim with boxes, bottles and crates.

According to historians, Berard introduced "peltries first, and followed up his commercial successes by the sale of fire-water to Indians…the little lake in Henrietta which bears his name is the only monument to his early visit and his stay, but there are many living who remember him well."

Berard lived so harmoniously with Native Americans that he "acquired the proprietorship of a squaw," wrote one historian. The 1840 census shows that his household included two people under the age of twenty. Since Berard was about fifty years old in 1840, these may have been his children.

In addition to the store, he also had a small farm where he raised wheat, corn and vegetables. He continued to live in this spot "long years after the last Pottawatomi disappeared from the county" and became "the last French trader known in Jackson County."

What happened to Berard? The last wishes of the Canadian who fell in love with Henrietta Township were to be laid to rest in his beloved township. The U.S. Find a Grave Index 1600s–Current shows John Baptiste Berrard, born in 1790, died in Jackson County on January 25, 1855. He was buried at Nims Cemetery near Pleasant Lake. The choice was particularly appropriate, since Pleasant Lake is a neighbor to the very lake that bears his name.[27]

HANKERD HOSPITALITY

The spirit of hospitality that emanated from Michael Hankerd's (1812–1861) beaming Irish eyes still lingers on the Hankerd homestead. Today, his property is the site of the Hankerd Inn Resort, a remodeled version of the 1857 original and an establishment that carries on a long tradition of cordiality.

It is likely that this genial tradition began in Ireland, where Michael was born in 1812. After all, Ireland is known as the Land of a Thousand Welcomes. But Michael's restless heart yearned for more than friendliness—he hankered for a place to flourish. So, in the 1830s, he left the Emerald Isle for the United States, immigrating first to New York and then moving to Michigan, where he worked for the Michigan Central Railroad.

While overseeing the building of railroad tracks between Detroit and Chelsea, Michael fell in love with Michigan's terrain and with Margaret Jones, a Michigan native whose family also emigrated from Ireland. The smitten Irishman married Margaret, left the railroad's employ and bought sixty acres in Dexter, where the couple settled. Their first home was a log cabin he built from scratch, including a large fireplace he fashioned from sticks and clay. The couple had four children, including son Patrick Hankerd (1845–1911), who showed an early interest in academics—a calling that would serve him well in adulthood.

In 1850, Michael moved his family to Jackson, where he bought 80 acres of land in Henrietta Township's section 17 on the southeastern end of Pleasant Lake. He ultimately acquired 325 acres of land, becoming one of the leading farming families. Patrick drove plows behind oxen teams as a boy, and in his spare time, he read and studied, becoming "one of the most widely informed young men in the community."

In 1857, the patriarch built a large brick residence that opened its doors to friends and visitors near and far. "Mr. Hankerd was a man of generous impulses, kindly and hospitable, and his door was always open to the passer by," said one biographer. One can almost smell a pot of stew simmering on the range and a loaf of Irish soda bread baking in the oven, ready for whoever may appear at the door.

Michael died in 1861, but his family carried on his cordial spirit and tenacious work ethic. Patrick worked as a teacher, was elected township clerk

Patrick and Sarah Hankerd originally owned the Hankerd homestead in Henrietta Township. *Courtesy Janet Rochefort.*

The Hankerd residence in Henritetta Township was known for its hospitality. *From Everts & Stewart Combination Atlas Map of Jackson County, 1874.*

in 1868 and served as township supervisor and a state legislator in the 1870s and 1880s. In 1872, Patrick married Sarah Birney, whose parents were early settlers in the area. The couple had eight children.

Historians were as complimentary of Patrick as they were of his father. They also recognized the social allure of the Hankerd homestead. One wrote, "Appreciating the great value of a popular resort, Mr. [Patrick] Hankerd has spent a great deal of money beautifying the grounds and adding to their attractiveness....To accommodate...visitors, he put up a fine new hotel and supplied it with all modern conveniences."

On September 11, 1911, the man with the ready smile and open door died. Patrick Hankerd was buried at Saints Cornelius and Cyprian Parish Cemetery in Leslie. But the story was not over. Drawn to the natural beauty of the spot, Jackson resident Janet Rochefort bought the Hankerd property in 1996 and opened it 1997 as the Hankerd Inn Resort, a bed-and-breakfast that carries on the long tradition of hospitality.

In 1996, Janet Rochefort bought the Hankerd property near Pleasant Lake and turned the homestead into a popular resort. *Courtesy Janet Rochefort.*

Among other transformations, Rochefort renovated the structure and expanded the complex to four buildings, providing a total of sixteen rooms and about twenty thousand square feet of space. The oldest building is a resurrected version of the 1857 original. Each room in the main house is named after a Hankerd family member and includes period antiques and objects reflecting their interests and occupations.

"If the original family members could visit it today, I think they'd be pleased," said Rochefort. "I'm doing what they would have done. Their spirit of hospitality lives on."[28]

17
Leoni Township

Fun Facts

- Leoni Township was organized in 1836 and was previously part of Napoleon and Henrietta Townships.
- One of the earliest settlers was Joseph H. Otis, who came from Vermont in 1830 with his step-sons, Zimri and Isaac Barber, and settled in sections 1 and 2. Other early settlers who came afterward included Joab Page, who built a sawmill in 1831; Norman Allen; Jacob Sagendorph; and Joel F. Parks.
- A post office was opened in the house of Moses Crowell in 1831. Ira J. Kellogg began construction on the first flour mill in 1832 and completed it in 1834. In 1835, John M. Whitwell began selling goods.
- The first school was opened in 1833, and Allen Knight was the first teacher.
- After the railroad pushed through Jackson County in the 1840s, trains would occasionally hit their grazing livestock, and rail officials took no responsibility. A small-scale war broke out between the railroad and Leoni's farmers. In 1850, a fire destroyed a Michigan Central Rail freight depot, leading to the arrests of fifty Leoni farmers and a conspiracy trial that remains one of the most fascinating episodes in railroad history.[29]

THE HIDDEN COMPARTMENT

Any remnant of the secret compartment where Seymour Treadwell (1795–1867) hid freedom seekers on his Leoni Township farm is lost to time—victim to the deterioration that occurs in most early to mid-1800s structures. But there is no question that this statesman, author and activist in the early Republican Party used his property to conceal enslaved Americans traveling on the Underground Railroad.

Evidence of Treadwell's participation did not emerge during his lifetime. The activist covered his tracks well, avoiding any proof of this clandestine activity. Decades after he died, however, his daughter wrote about his secret life—and the secret compartment—in her memoir, confirming what everyone had suspected for generations.

Treadwell's story began in Bridgeport, Connecticut, where he was born in 1795, the youngest child of a Revolutionary War veteran. He married Eliza Hartwell in 1819 in New York, where he ran a school, farmed and opened a bookshop. He wrote that his "conversion to immediate and universal emancipation of all who are in bonds without crime, was not a rash and an inconsiderate matter…since the first recollection of my childhood I have abhorred the oppressor and sympathized with the oppressed."

Treadwell rose to national acclaim in 1837, when he delivered an Independence Day address to an antislavery group in New York. The speech was so stirring that supporters urged him to write a book about his abolition arguments. One year later, he published *American Liberties and American Slavery Morally and Politically Illustrated*. It was a systematic rebuttal of the most common objections to abolition and a best seller in the North. (The book is still available for purchase online.)

Seymour B. Treadwell of Leoni was an author and Underground Railroad activist. *Sketch by Brianne Witt, assistant art professor, Spring Arbor University, courtesy Linda Hass.*

Treadwell's national renown brought him to the attention of the Michigan Anti-Slavery Society, which invited him to "come to Michigan as editor and lecturer for the Society." In 1839, the passionate orator made a preliminary address in

Jackson; it was so well received that he accepted an offer to move there, ultimately farming in Leoni Township.

Almost every aspect of Treadwell's energetic life revolved around the eradication of slavery. He served as president of the Michigan Anti-Slavery Society, helped lay the antislavery groundwork for the formation of the Republican Party and spent several months touring with former freedom seeker Henry Bibb. Bibb wrote about their adventures, and about Treadwell's zeal and support, in his autobiography, *The Life and Adventurers of Henry Bibb, An American Slave*.

For all these reasons and more, most people suspected that Treadwell also participated in the Underground Railroad, but there was no proof until his daughter, Isabel Treadwell Towne, penned her memoirs. She revealed that her father "did not allow farming to interfere with this antislavery work. His fine new barn, still standing in Leoni, was a station of the Underground Rail Road [*sic*]."

Towne also visited Jackson's library toward the end of her life. A stenographer typed a transcript of Towne's recollections during the visit. For the first time, listeners learned where the secret compartment was located. According to the typed excerpt, Treadwell's barn floor had a trapdoor that, when opened, led to the hiding place. In this concealed basement, which was likely dark and dank—but at least safe—freedom seekers waited for the next leg of their journey to Canada. An 1858 map of Jackson County shows Treadwell's Leoni Township property was bounded by Seymour and Hawkins Roads, which exist by those names today.

Seymour Treadwell died on June 9, 1867. Shortly before he died, he was visited by the renowned abolitionist Wendell Phillips, who congratulated him on his contributions toward a "hard-fought battle." Treadwell's obituary stated the "great work of his life" was to "do what he could toward the abolition of slavery." He was buried at Mt. Evergreen Cemetery and is one of eight people mentioned on a Michigan Historical Marker honoring Underground Railroad activists buried in the cemetery. While Treadwell's special compartment remained concealed during his lifetime, he would likely be glad to know it is openly celebrated today.[30]

THE GREAT RAILROAD CONSPIRACY

One of the most fascinating railroad conspiracies in the nation involved a charismatic Leoni Township resident who fought the Michigan Central Railroad (MCRR) in the mid-1850s—and lost. The episode, known as the Great Railroad Conspiracy, may not be new to some readers, since it is still studied by legal experts. What would be new, however, is learning the secret occupation of the figure at the center of the story, Captain Abel F. Fitch, a major property owner whose livestock were among those killed by fast-moving trains.

Able Fitch of Leoni was entangled in the Great Railroad Conspiracy. *Sketch by Brianne Witt, assistant art professor, Spring Arbor University, courtesy Linda Hass.*

This sad tale of intrigue, love and loss began when trains hit grazing livestock as the locomotives steamed through Jackson County. Farmers, who lost up to 160 head along a twelve-mile stretch, saw the trains as iron interlopers roaring through their quiet pasture lands, disturbing the peace and slaughtering their cattle, sheep and hogs. They sued rail officials but were only reimbursed for half of their losses. Faced with what farmers called "legalized robbery," they struck back, piling lumber, rocks and other obstacles on the rails. Occasionally, they would even shoot at trains.

Jackson County became the heart of a small-scale war against the MCRR, led by Fitch, a Leoni Township supervisor and former captain of a cavalry company known as the Barry Horse Guards. Fitch, a fervent spokesman for the farmers, warned railroad officials to "take responsibility" for their actions.

The railroad responded by offering a reward for anyone who could provide incriminating evidence leading to the conviction of those sabotaging their rails. It also hired spies to catch farmers in the act of vandalism. Unable to do so, some historians now believe the railroad's hired hands set fire to the MCRR's Detroit freight depot, burning it to the ground so they could falsely accuse the farmers and collect the reward.

Although the railroad's star witness was a convicted horse thief, his allegations were sufficient for authorities to sweep into Jackson in April

1851, round up fifty residents, including Fitch, and cart them off to a Detroit prison. The resulting trial, known as the Great Railroad Conspiracy, got underway in the summer of 1851, attracting the attention of William H. Seward, a former New York governor and future secretary of state under Abraham Lincoln. Seward, a lawyer and renowned figure, sympathized with the Jacksonians and agreed to represent Fitch and fellow defendants.

Although the source of the blaze was never determined, twelve conspirators were convicted in September 1851. None, however, completed his prison terms, and the others were ultimately pardoned. Any pardon Fitch might have received would have come too late for the Leoni Township resident, who did not fare well in the squalid prison. On August 25, 1851, aware that he would not live, Fitch called his wife, Amanda, to him, took her hand and, pressing it to his lips, said, "Amanda, it is hard to part! I die of a broken heart!" He died a few days later and was buried at Jackson's Mt. Evergreen Cemetery.

His tombstone simply gives his name, death date and age of forty-three years. What it does not say is that among Fitch's accomplishments, this cavalry captain, prosperous farmer, township supervisor and former postmaster was also an Underground Railroad activist. Battle Creek stationmaster Erastus Hussey named Fitch among those in his network in an interview after slavery was abolished.

Not much else is known about Fitch's secret occupation, but the disclosure contributes to a clearer picture of the historical figure. Behind closed doors and under the radar, this bold yet compassionate soul was a secret champion of the downtrodden. His premature death is a poignant reminder that not all of Jackson's history has a happy ending, except perhaps posthumously, as readers can develop a greater appreciation for the historical figure at the center of the greatest of all railroad conspiracies.[31]

18
Liberty Township

Fun Facts

- The first settler in Liberty Township was Moses Tuthill, who arrived in 1835 and built the first frame barn in 1838 and the first frame house in 1839. Other early settlers included John Neely, John Hess, Jesse Bivins and Nathaniel Pettengill.
- Residents met in the house of Solomon Skill to organize the township in 1837. After much discussion, the name "Liberty" was unanimously accepted.
- The first sawmill was built by Mr. Otto in 1837 on section 23 on the Grand River. The first flour mill was built by Erastus Fuller in 1848 on section 26, also on the Grand River. The first school was taught by Nancy Tuttle in 1838 in the home of Solomon Skiff. She had between twelve and fifteen students. The first post office was established in 1838. Franklin Pierce was the first postmaster, bringing mail from Brooklyn on foot once a week.
- Liberty Township contains one of the headwaters of the Grand River, which measures 252 miles from its source to Lake Michigan. It is the longest river in Michigan and the geographic divide between rivers flowing west to Lake Michigan and east to Lake Erie.[32]

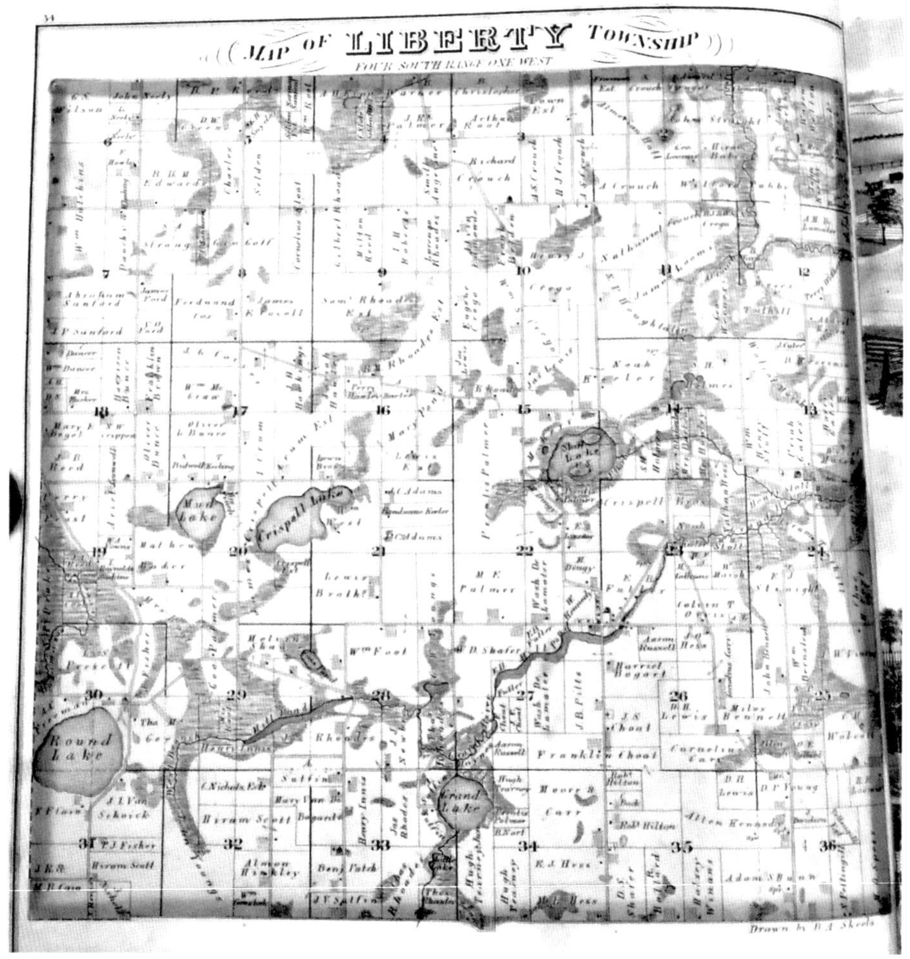

From Everts & Stewart Combination Atlas Map of Jackson County, 1874.

GENUINE FRONTIER LIFE

In the iconic movie *The Wizard of Oz*, Dorothy and her companions cry out, "Lions, tigers and bears, oh my!" If those predators were the only obstacles the Pettengill family faced when they moved to Liberty Township in 1835, members would have rejoiced. As it was, their survival was threatened by snakes, wolves, bears, prairie fires and much more in the rugged terrain—all of which made for incredible tales.

Nathan Pettengill (1799–1878); his wife, Sophia (1804–1882); and their four children moved from Andover, Vermont, to Michigan in 1835, where they settled on section 13 of Liberty Township. They built a twelve-foot-square log hut with a thatched hay roof and a fireplace.

In many ways, their experiences seem tailor-made for a movie about travel to another world. Every spring, when Native Americans set the prairie on fire, the Pettengills would scramble through the haze to rake brush away from the house, douse the surrounding ground with water and hope the leaping flames missed their property.

On Sundays, the family walked ten miles round trip to church, often driving wolves from their path. When the predators weren't shadowing them through the woods, they were serenading them at night. Over time, the family could recognize individual wolves by their distinctive howls. According to their recollections, the howling concerts came regularly with nightfall: "A heavy coarse voice leading, a shriller one following, and the 10 tenors joining in the chorus. They ceased at the close of their vespers in orderly fashion, the oldest desisting first, and so on, until the music ended in the final squeal of a youngster."

The Pettengill family from Liberty Township built and lived in a log cabin similar to this one. *Author's photo, Ella Sharp Museum, Jackson.*

The Pettengills were alternately alarmed, interested and amused by the wolves' performances. There was no amusement, however, when a den of blue racers threatened them. Family members killed all but one of the snakes, and the lone assailant continued to strike. According to a biographer, that serpent also met his doom: "His snakeship landed in the branches and gave battle, stretching several feet in the air....Finally he flung himself toward the eldest son, a boy about 11 years old, who hit him as he flew through the air and killed him. He [the snake] was seven feet long, the average length of the entire lot."

One of their more amusing encounters was when Nathaniel and his son William encountered a bear while searching for cows at dusk. Father and son quickly hid in the bushes. When the unsuspecting beast reached the top of a knoll, William sprang out, alarming the animal so much that it lost its balance and spiraled backward down the hill, rolling over and over in somersaults. Finally, it plunged into some brushwood before disappearing for good.

Not all animals were annoying or threatening—some were lifesaving, especially when it came to delivering food. In the early years, food was unpredictable and sometimes unattainable. The family became so desperate at one point that they cut wheat before it matured and boiled it for food. Another time, their diet consisted entirely of potatoes and salt, with the potatoes hauled by ox teams from Monroe. The biographer wrote that en route the oxen would trudge through the mud, sinking up to their sides, or lumber through forest fires, "singeing the hair off the poor beasts."

The family survived these challenges and looked back on their trials and tribulations with a bit of nostalgia. Their long-forgotten recollections are a testament to the endurance of pioneers and reflect a lifestyle that seems foreign to readers today. But it was, as the Pettengills said, a slice of "genuine frontier life."[33]

Historical Roots of South Jackson Community Church

When William and Sarah Ann Root deeded land for a church in 1875, they had no idea their gift would evolve into something that set norms, helped the needy and inspired stained-glass beauty—but it did. Over the decades, their gift blossomed into the South Jackson Community Church, a faith community that accomplished all that and more. The church building and property at 1024 West Kimmel Road sits on the border of Liberty and Summit Townships and includes a historical cemetery with its own fascinating story.

In 1837, however, the congregation had no formal building, existing as an expression of worship that took place in private homes. By 1849, members decided the time had come for an official meetinghouse, so they constructed a twenty-four-by-thirty-foot log building for gatherings. The church was first called the Baptist Church of South Jackson and later the Baptist Church of South Jackson and Liberty.

The structure sat on property originally owned by a family who deeded the property to William and Amy Root in 1850. The Roots, in turn, deeded one acre to the Baptist Church. William Root (1816–1888) was a farmer, blacksmith and church deacon for many years. Amy Root (1817–1854) was known by various first names, including Anna, Amy and Sarah Ann. The couple was buried at South Jackson Cemetery.

Early church members took their calling so seriously that on October 4, 1851, they appointed a committee to visit "Sister Crawford" and express their displeasure at her "visiting dancing parties, balls and dancing." The rough-hewn building continued to serve as a meetinghouse for the congregation, mostly Liberty Township residents, until 1876, when it was destroyed by fire. The disaster prompted a log entry from an exasperated church clerk: "I make this sad record…between the hours of 12 and 1 of night, the meeting house of the Baptist Church…was burned! No doubt it was set on fire by some person. May he never die or have any peace until he shall confess the awful crime!"

In the face of this disaster, William Root once again stepped in to offer encouragement in the form of an additional deed of land encompassing 1.19 acres. The congregation matched his optimism by building a thirty-foot-by-forty-foot wood frame structure with a tall steeple. The stately white building with its hand-carved beams and pews, reminiscent of New England churches, was dedicated on February 13, 1879. An adjoining parcel of land was deeded to the church by Arvilla Lewis in 1889.

Records show that the congregation was socially active, forming a Whatsoever Aid Society in 1887 to help the needy. From 1896 to 1949, the church ceased official operations, but many women remained active by sewing quilts and baking goods to cover maintenance costs. Members today believe that a circular antique rose window in front of the narthex was installed in 1878 at the church's rededication following the fire. In

Above: South Jackson Community Church in Jackson was dedicated in 1879, but the congregation was formed in 1837. *Author's photo.*

Left: Martha Welch Crispell's distinctive tombstone displays a tub and washboard—tools of her trade. She was buried at South Jackson Community Church Cemetery. *Author's photo.*

1948, record-keeping resumed under the name South Jackson Community Church. The nondenominational church holds services to this day.

The neighboring cemetery, called God's Acre by early congregants, predates the church and has its own interesting history. Fascinating clues on grave markers are likely missed by passing motorists. Those who stop and search, however, will find intriguing hints about the lives of early congregants—not on paper but etched in the granite and marble markers.

The oldest marker is that of William Thompson, who died in 1840 at the age of 102. Several markers honor Civil War veterans. Among the more interesting monuments is that of Martha Welch Crispell, who died in 1870. The tall, vertical monument depicts a scrub board, tub and air dryer with the inscription "Gone from her industry."

According to the census and other records, Martha was born in 1791 in New York, moved to Michigan and married John Crispell. The couple lived in Liberty Township. Relatives said she was a weaver and used the tub for dyeing fabric. It was a calling that apparently defined her life and now, thanks to the decorative tombstone, identifies her in death.

Many believe the church's enduring presence and historic roots are a source of inspiration extending into the future. "The same year Michigan became a state, a firm foundation was laid here at South Jackson Community Church for the future of our families, our community, and state," said church pastor Steve Brown. Indeed, that foundation not only stretches back generations, but it also supports a church that continues to blossom today.[34]

19

Napoleon Township

Fun Facts

- A.B. Goodwin was the first settler in the area in 1832. Other early settlers included Chauncey and Lyman Hawley, Samuel Quigley, Harvey Austin and Roswell Rexford.
- The first post office in the area was established in 1832. The first merchants were John and C.C. Dewey in 1835.
- The first teacher was Louisa Swain in 1833, who taught in the house of Samuel Quigley. The first district school was built in 1835.
- Abraham Bolton and Roswell Rexford were delegates to the Constitutional Convention held in 1836, which created the constitution for the State of Michigan in 1837.
- After undergoing several boundary changes, Napoleon Township was set apart as a separate township in 1859. The township was named after Napoleon Bonaparte, the infamous military leader and ruler in France, at the request of resident Abram Bolton.[35]

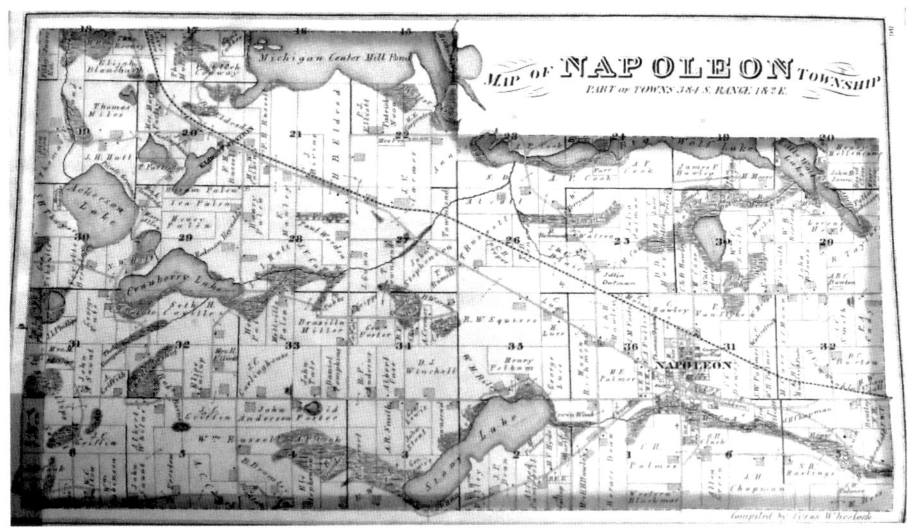

From Everts & Stewart Combination Atlas Map of Jackson County, 1874.

FREEMAN CROSBY—HEALER AND PATRIOT

Imagine undergoing an operation by a surgeon who attended a year or two of college with no formal surgical or laboratory instruction—and whose anesthesia of choice was chloroform. Now imagine *that* surgeon is far superior to the alternative.

Napoleon Township's Dr. Freeman R. Crosby (1828–1895) represented that superior medical choice in the mid-1800s. Crosby, whose credentials might alarm today's patients, was better educated than most doctors and was a selfless servant when it came to serving his country and treating generations of Napoleon residents.

Crosby was born in Lewis County, New York, in 1828, the son of Jonathan and Charlotte Crosby. In 1838, his family moved to Napoleon, where his father was a farmer. Young Crosby "was educated in common schools and reared on a farm." His aptitude for science soared well beyond common schools, and he set his sights on the University of Michigan's medical school. Fortunately for him, most medical schools of the time required only "a year of college, a high school education, or its equivalent."

In 1858, Crosby apprenticed under a doctor, and from 1859 through 1860, he attended courses and lectures at the University of Michigan. Historians say this path was typical of the time, since most medical students received little to no surgical instruction, serving as apprentices in lieu of formal training. In addition, few medical students actually graduated from college in the mid-1800s. Typically, they attended two or four semesters of classes, supplemented by lectures. But even lecture attendance was limited to those who could afford the ticket price, since speakers' incomes were augmented by ticket sales. The University of Michigan's catalogue of graduates and non-graduates confirms that Crosby attended the school.

After the Civil War began, the rookie doctor enlisted in Company S of Michigan's Seventeenth Infantry Regiment in 1862, serving as an assistant surgeon under Dr. J.D. Bevier. The most common surgery during the Civil War was amputation, often necessitated by the destructive Minié ball bullet, which shattered bones and limbs. About 90 percent of all surgeries in the Civil War involved ether or chloroform as the chosen anesthesia, with the latter killing patients if administered in too high of a dose.

Crosby probably had more opportunities to practice amputation and anesthesia than he would have liked. Among other experiences, he served in the Battle of Fredericksburg, which resulted in about 13,000 Union casualties, and the Battle of Vicksburg, which resulted in about 4,800 Union casualties. Field doctors were often awash in pools of blood as they performed operations near stacks of amputated limbs.

A weary Dr. Crosby was mustered out of service in 1864 and returned to the pastoral peace of Napoleon Township, where he continued to practice

Dr. Freeman Crosby from Napoleon was a Civil War surgeon who often worked under dangerous conditions. *Author's photo, Jackson Civil War Muster.*

medicine. In 1865, at the age of thirty-seven, he married Nancy Andrews. The couple had two children, one of whom died in infancy. Crosby is listed in the U.S. censuses of 1870 and 1880 as a doctor in Napoleon. In 1893, like many war veterans, he was appointed postmaster of Napoleon Township.

In 1895, the patriot who served his country admirably in the Civil War and who treated and healed generations of Napoleon residents was laid to rest at Oak Grove Cemetery in Napoleon Township.[36]

THE SECRET LIFE OF ROSWELL REXFORD

When renowned abolitionist Laura Haviland needed money to help a former slave start a business in Michigan, she turned to Major Roswell B. Rexford (1805–1863) of Napoleon Township. According to historians, the wealthy farmer not only financed the Underground Railroad but also used his home and barn as a refuge for passengers, although his secret life was hidden from the average resident.

Born in New York, Rexford, his wife and children settled in Napoleon in 1832. By day, Rexford ran a successful 160-acre farm along what is now M-50, south of Napoleon. By night, the free-spirited idealist opened the doors of his stately brick home to the south-northeast branch of the Underground Railroad. This branch came from northern Indiana into Adrian, where Haviland and her husband, Charles Haviland, lived and operated the famous Raisin Institute—the first racially integrated school in Michigan.

Haviland not only taught at the institute but also secured financial assistance on behalf of her students, which prompted her to write to Rexford in 1860. She sought funding for a self-freed blacksmith from Louisiana who needed seed money to start his own business in Michigan. Rexford's generous reply was so touching that she included it in her autobiography.

Rexford wrote that he was "glad to learn that another has escaped from the land of bondage, whips and chains....I would rather enter the gloomy cell...and spend every hour of this brief existence in all the bitterness that the hand of tyrants can inflict, than live in the pomp and splendor that the unpaid toil of slaves could lavish upon a man."

Rexford's participation in the Underground Railroad was unknown to most but apparently acknowledged by some. Nellie Blair Greene, daughter of Michigan Civil War governor Austin Blair, wrote in the August 23, 1924

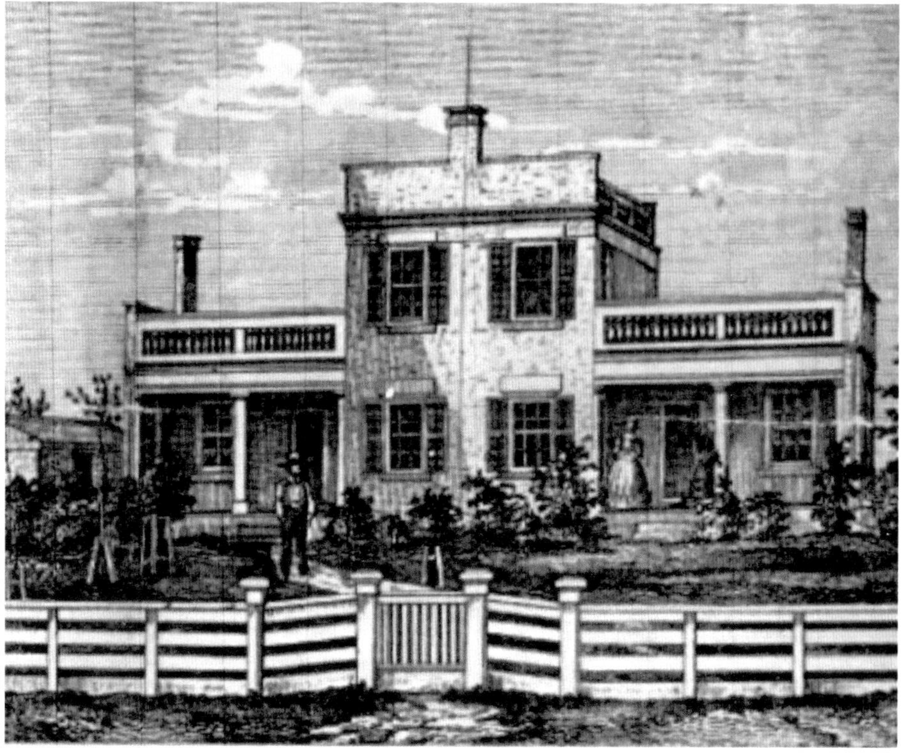

The residence of Roswell Rexford in Napoleon served as a safe house on the Underground Railroad. *From Jos. Alexander Map of Jackson County, Mich., 1858.*

issue of the *Jackson Citizen Patriot* that "during the days of the Underground Railroad, one of the stations on this humanitarian line was situated on the Rexford farm, the barns being planned especially for the reception of fugitive slaves from southern states."

A Rexford descendant quoted in the February 27, 1946 issue of the *Jackson Citizen Patriot* recounted a story passed down through the generations in which an ancestor came down from the upstairs bedroom one morning to see "slaves that were smuggled by the 'underground railroad' from the south to freedom in Canada."

Rexford was active in his faith and politics. In 1834, he helped found the Napoleon Baptist Church, and in 1835, he won a runoff election as one of two delegates to attend a Constitutional Convention in which the language of Michigan's first constitution was hammered out. In 1859, he was chosen as Napoleon's first supervisor during the township's first election. While no record of him serving in the U.S. military has been found, his title as "major" may refer to a position with the Michigan militia, which was approved as part of the state's first constitution.

In 1863, the activities of this busy deacon, farmer and humanitarian came to an end. He was laid to rest at Oak Grove Cemetery in Napoleon. His obituary stated, "Mr. R. was a man that commanded the respect and esteem of all who knew him....A good man and a useful citizen has gone." One of those uses, we now know, was to help enslaved Americans pass from their bonds into freedom.[37]

20

Norvell Township

Fun Facts

- Among the first settlers on land that is now Norvell Township was William Hunt in 1831. The next year, his son-in-law, Mr. Bickford, arrived. A daughter was born shortly thereafter, becoming the first child born to settlers in the township. She was known not only for this distinction, but also for her lengthy name: Dona Maria Cassender Rider Bickford.
- The township was named after John Norvell, one of Michigan's first U.S. senators, who resided in Detroit.
- A post office was established on land that is now Norvell Township in 1837, with Harvey Austin serving as the first postmaster.
- After undergoing many changes, the present boundaries of Norvell Township were established in 1873.[38]

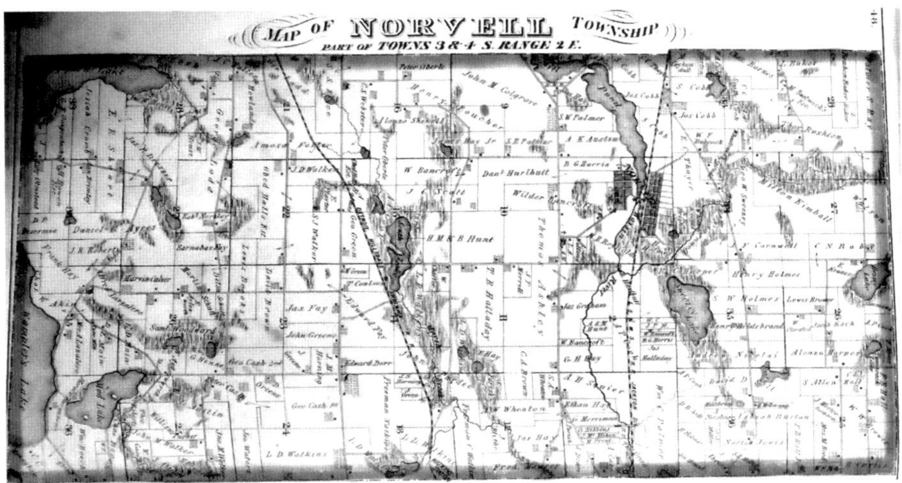

From Everts & Stewart Combination Atlas Map of Jackson County, 1874.

THE SOUTHERN POSSE AND THE DEFIANT FARMER

If your house was surrounded by an armed posse, would you venture outside or barricade yourself inside? Norvell Township resident Royal Watkins faced that choice in 1847. His response was so extraordinary that it was included in the autobiography of a renowned historical figure. Such a conflict was likely the last thing on his mind, however, when he first beheld the peaceful "solemn grandeur" of Norvell Township.

Royal Watkins (1788–1876) was born in Keene, New Hampshire, where he was "reared among the southern hills" with extended family who fought for America's independence. It is a heritage that hints at the family's backbone in dealing with conflict. Royal supplemented his practical education by reading, ultimately becoming a teacher as well as a farmer.

After marrying Sally Carpenter, Royal investigated land in the Michigan Territory and found what he was looking for in section 13 of what is today Norvell Township. In 1834, the couple packed their bags and set off for their new home. Royal's son, Lucius Watkins, later wrote about the journey, stating that the family departed on April 9 and traveled by wagon across land to Buffalo, New York, where they took a steamboat across the Erie Canal to Detroit. There, they bought supplies, two wagons and four oxen to carry the load, arriving at their property, a picturesque setting they would later call Fairview Farm, on May 10. Lucius wrote about the location in his memoir, stating, "No pen can describe the park-like plains and rolling openings or the solemn grandeur of the timber lands. No ear will again hear the howl of the wolf or the scream of the panther....We were nearly in the center of the wilderness about 10 miles in diameter....The upland was covered in luxuriant grass and was the natural home of the deer, bear, wolf, panther, lynx and wildcat."

Fairview Farm prospered, thanks to the wise management of father and son and the workers they hired, including John White, who had escaped from a Kentucky plantation in 1847. White was initially harbored by abolitionist Laura Haviland, who referred him to Royal's farm in neighboring Norvell Township. All went well for Royal and the field hand until John's former plantation owner, George Brazier, decided to reclaim his "property."

Brazier hired Kentucky lawyer J.L. Smith to launch a raid into Michigan. The dynamics that led the wily lawyer to Haviland's farm in the fall of 1847 were described at length in Haviland's autobiography. She wrote that Smith posed as an Ohio schoolteacher, feigned interest in her "excellent school" and said he wanted to know more about "underground railroad projects" for a magazine he supposedly represented. He fooled no one, least of all Haviland.

Following Smith's visit, a "tide of excitement" swept over the Haviland household. She suspected that White was the real object of Smith's visit and decided to warn White and Royal of "imminent" danger. She grabbed one of her horses and sent a "dispatch bearer" to the Watkins's farm. Would the rider arrive in time?

Meanwhile, in Norvell Township, Smith and a posse armed with pistols and Bowie knives raced to Watkins's farm, where they apprehended an unsuspecting field hand working outside. On discovering that he was not the object of their search, the intruders surrounded Watkins's log cabin. The posse leader pounded on the door, demanded the owner "show himself" and produce their "slave." One can only guess what the mob expected to find—perhaps a compliant northerner who acquiesced to the demands? What the members found instead was a defiant fifty-two-year-old farmer who not only stepped out of his house but also took control of his domain.

Royal's reply was ultimately relayed to Haviland, who preserved it for posterity in her autobiography. Royal told the posse, "There are others, myself included, who are ready to do as much to save a self-freed man from being taken back to Southern bondage." Then looking the posse leader square in the eye, he added, "We have a law here to arrest and take care of men who make such threats as you have here."

Top: Royal and Lucius Watkins owned one of the premier farms in Norvell Township. *From Everts & Stewart Combination Atlas Map of Jackson County, 1874.*

Bottom: Royal Watkins, an Underground Railroad activist in Norvell Township, once defied a southern posse who surrounded his property in 1847. *Author's photo.*

But the trump card had yet to been played. Haviland's dispatch rider did reach Watkins ahead of time, and the farmer had responded to the warning by taking White to Jackson's train depot, where White traveled (likely undercover) on the first train to Detroit. In short, the object of the posse's search was long gone.

HISTORIC AMTRAK STATION

Most Jacksonians are familiar with the historical Amtrak station at 501 East Michigan Avenue, the oldest continuously operating railroad-designed-and-built passenger station in the United States. The depot opened with much fanfare in 1873 and remains an enduring landmark to this day.

But if the station was constructed in 1873, how could Underground Railroad activists have used it in the mid-1840s? The depot's history actually dates to 1841, when the Michigan Central Railroad (MCRR) first reached Jacksonburg from Detroit. The original local depot, a humble wood frame building operated by Collins, Hahn & Dalziel Coal Co. as early as 1841, was located at the intersection of East Michigan Avenue and Columbus Street, near the current depot. Over the years, the railroad underwent many changes, consolidations and the construction of different freight stations and car repair shops. By 1871, Jackson had more passengers traveling through it than any other city in the state, transforming the town into a rail transportation hub.

To offer a station worthy of such standing, MCRR turned to H.R. Gardener, a master builder for the railroads, to create a "grand central station." The resulting Victorian Italianate–style building at 501 East Michigan Avenue was finished in 1873. In 2002, the depot was added to the National Register of Historic Places. It remains an enduring landmark with a fascinating legacy.*

Jackson's Amtrak station is the oldest continuously operating railroad-designed-and-built passenger station in the United States. *Courtesy Jackson District Library.*

* *Jackson Daily Citizen*, June 18, 1872; August 26, 1873; Leanne Smith, "Peek Through Time: Jackson's Amtrak Station Is Still Going Strong After 137 Years," May 7, 2010; Ken Wyatt, "Peek Through Time: Central Railroad Shops Tell of Jackson's Rise and Fall as a Railroad Town," June 7, 2018.

With that, the high-stakes poker game between the posse and the defiant farmer had come to an end. White successfully made it to Canada, as evidence proves, and Smith returned to Kentucky empty-handed. Although there would be other fights and even lawsuits between Michigan abolitionists and southern slave owners in years to come, on this day, Royal emerged as the true king of his domain.

Royal later expanded his estate, built an Italianate brick house with a prominent lookout tower and passed the reins of the estate to his son, Lucius. On July 18, 1876, after a long and successful life, the Norvell Township farmer who stood his ground against a Kentucky posse died. Royal Watkins was buried at Oak Grove Cemetery in Manchester.[39]

THE WEARY WANDERER

If you had to walk 255 miles in the wilderness to check out prospective property, would you do it? James Graham (1803–1890) endured this hardship and much more to stake his claim on eighty acres of land in Norvell Township in 1832. His plight underscores the relative ease today's motorists have in traveling from location to location, thanks to highways, road signs and global positioning satellites. There were no such conveniences in Graham's day, when a trail in the wilderness could quickly become unrecognizable.

Such was the case when Graham, son of an Irish immigrant, set out from Detroit to Jackson in May 1832. If he walked the distance, which he likely did, that would have added another seventy-three miles to his total. His mode of transportation to Jackson is unknown, but once there, he spent Sunday night with Napoleon pioneers William Hunt and D. Goodrich. The next day, Graham set out on foot for Marshall, intent on investigating property there.

The only pathway leading to his destination was a Native American trail that cut through the wilderness. These trails would often intersect others, branching off in various directions like a spiderweb on the ground. It took a keen eye to spot the fallen branch that marked intersections, as long as the branch hadn't moved, or the worn foot paths, if they hadn't become overgrown. Travelers had to catch all these clues while keeping an eye out for predators, including wolves and bears.

Along the way, Graham's feet were willing, but his eyes were weak. It was a weary wanderer who ended up twenty-five miles south of Marshall by Tuesday evening. What to do? Determined, Graham turned around and backtracked until he finally reached Marshall by Wednesday afternoon. During the journey, he "dined on two crackers" and, at night, rested his body "beneath the clear sky on bare ground." Clearly, this Irishman was not about to give up.

In Marshall, Graham stayed with acquaintances; checked out available property; and, for reasons unspecified, decided to head back to Jackson—on foot. By intention or mistake, he arrived in what is now Norvell Township and beheld the property of his dreams—a rolling landscape covered in hardwoods, meadows and wetlands. Finally, the weary wanderer had found his home. He picked out an eighty-acre section and set out to register his claim—again on foot. It is not known how many pairs of shoes or boots he wore out, but one thing is clear: this Irishman had very sturdy feet.

With property in his possession, he returned to his home, Waterville, New York, where he married Vanlara Tyler of the same village. The couple lived there for three years before moving to Detroit in the spring of 1835. Did they choose Graham's trademark form of transportation from Detroit to the Norvell property? Possibly. Once they arrived, Graham's feet got no rest as he went to work building the couple's log cabin and planting crops. What he might have lacked in exploration savvy, he more than made up for in determination and strength, improving his farm "until it was as fine a farm as any in the county," said his biographer.

Vanlara died in 1838. The couple had one son. In 1840, Graham married Paulina Allen, with whom he had six more children. He enjoyed a successful life and called Norvell home until the end of his days. In 1890, the weary traveler rested his feet for good. He was laid to rest in Norvell Cemetery. James Graham had endured the wilderness, near starvation and predators to live to the ripe old age of eighty-seven. He is among the unsung pioneers who saw Norvell Township's potential and did his part to develop it.[40]

21

Parma Township

Fun Facts

- Parma Township was organized in 1837. The first township meeting was held at the house of John Graham that same year. John Barnum was elected supervisor.
- The first permanent settler was Elihu Gould in 1832, although in 1831, George Ketchum purchased the first land, which was not settled immediately. Ketchum's property was later known as Ball's Tavern, named after a large wooden ball that he placed on a tamarack pole.
- The first railroad station in this vicinity, known as Gidley's Station, was opened in 1845 on the Michigan Central Railroad line.
- In 1866, a fire almost destroyed the entire village of Parma.
- The village of Parma was originally called Groveland, but the name was changed to Parma in 1849. Unofficially, Parma was known as Cracker Hill for years. The village was incorporated in 1864.
- The first store in Parma was built by William Kassick in 1846, and the first warehouse was built by Isaac Cushman in 1848.[41]

From Everts & Stewart Combination Atlas Map of Jackson County, 1874.

QUAKERTOWN

An intriguing bronze plaque on a large boulder sits at a lonely intersection sandwiched between cornfields and barns in Parma Township. Few notice the plaque, except perhaps an occasional car and a cow or two. But in the 1830s, this spot at the intersection of Devereaux and Gibbs Roads marked a lively little town known by the uniqueness of its residents, who were Quakers.

According to the bronze plaque, Quakers, also known as "Friends," began migrating to this spot around 1835. As more joined the settlement, some Jacksonians began referring to it as a "Quaker colony." One Jackson historian whose mother was of Quaker stock said the colony reached out to his family around 1835–36. He wrote, "Among the early settlers...mostly in the town of Parma, were several families of Quakers or Friends....My mother was of Quaker stock...and by some strange instinct the colony sought her out....I can remember when a boy of riding to Parma after an ox team to visit our Quaker friends."

By 1839, the settlement, also known as Hickory Grove, boasted a log schoolhouse and a post office, with John Mott serving as the first postmaster. Mott, an educated man, also founded and operated Mott Seminary, a nearby coeducational boarding school. He was joined by fellow Quakers Isaac and Uriah Mott, George and William Hoag and Samuel and Edward Upton, to name a few.

By 1844, the Quaker community organized a Hickory Grove monthly meeting, built a meetinghouse and established a nearby burying ground, known as Friends of Hickory Grove Cemetery. Many of the aged tombstones

A Quaker colony thrived near this spot in Parma Township in the 1830s. Today, the colony is memorialized by a bronze marker. *Author's photo.*

are still in good enough shape to depict the carving of an index finger pointing up, symbolizing the hope of heaven.

The Quaker meetinghouse, the center of interest and activity, was a simple one-room building. An early local newspaper article described a typical Quaker meeting: "On one side of the room sat the men solemnly, wearing their wide brimmed hats; on the other side…sat the women in their grey gowns and kerchiefs. No word was spoken, deep quiet prevailed, and only the bird songs were heard through the open windows. Suddenly, the Spirit would move one of those good men, and he would rise to his feet and speak fervently and sincerely his message. Perhaps another would feel this inward urge to voice some thought. There was no friction; everything was peaceful and pleasant."

Over the years, the community disbanded for unknown reasons, the post office closed and the spot quietly slipped into posterity. Around 1878, the log schoolhouse was replaced by a wood frame building that has since served generations of children and a 4-H Club. A few remnants of this once-vital settlement remain, though, including street signs bearing the names of former Quaker landowners and a bronze plaque affixed to a boulder. The plaque, on the northwest side of the intersection, memorializes the spot as the former Quakertown. Perhaps the invisible footprint of these devout souls remains stamped on the soil, as well.[42]

Where Are They Now?

While many Quakers left Parma Township around 1860, some remained. According to U.S. censuses, Thomas Mott, founder of a Quakertown seminary, still resided in Parma in 1850, but by 1860, he and his wife, Mary, had returned to their native New York. A relative, Isaac Mott, also lived in Parma in 1850, but by 1860, he and his wife, Mary, had moved to Battle Creek, where he worked as a "nursery man." George Hoag, who was born in Parma in 1847, remained there. The U.S. censuses from 1850 through 1900 show that Hoag worked as a farmer. He died in 1909 and was buried at Parma Cemetery. Today, Hoag Street in Parma bears witness to his family's presence.

FROM PANAMA TO PARMA

Napoleon B. Graham (1825–1890) had some serious soul-searching and wandering to do before he found his place in the world. When he finally did, that place was none other than his hometown in Parma Township. Perhaps wanderlust was part of his DNA, after all, his paternal grandfather, Samuel Graham, was restless enough to emigrate from Scotland to America in the 1770s. Even after the patriarch arrived here, however, he yearned for something more—freedom and a wide-open country he could call his own. So, Samuel joined the American Revolution and fought on the side of the colonists.

Napoleon's father, John Graham, inherited that restless spirit and ended up traveling to Michigan in 1831 to buy 640 acres in sections 31 and 32 of Parma Township at $1.25 per acre. After building a twenty-foot-by-twenty-five-foot log cabin for his family of ten, the entrepreneur built a tavern that became the first regular public house in the township. It was also the site of the first town meeting, and it hosted the first township ball, drawing people from near and far.

Napoleon, who was born in 1825, assisted his father in these and other building projects and spent his boyhood attending school during the winter and plowing, sowing and reaping crops the rest of the year. As busy as this kept the young Napoleon, it was not enough. Like his namesake, he yearned for more. There were new horizons to conquer and greener pastures to explore. Perhaps he was tired of his farm chores. Or maybe he inherited a touch of the Graham wanderlust. For whatever reason, he yearned for a change.

In 1847, Napoleon married Mary Pierce in Parma. The couple settled down in the township, but by 1852, distant horizons beckoned. His biographer simply states, "In 1852 he was seized with the California gold fever." Seeking fame and riches, he assembled a team and a covered wagon and started across the plains. Presumably, Mary went with him. The team traveled in this way during the entire 2,500-mile trip, camping out "wherever night overtook them, with the journey occupying four months."

Napoleon spent over a year in pursuit of glittering possibilities. Noticeably absent, however, is any mention of the young explorer ever finding what he was after. Finally, weariness set in, and the vagabond experienced a yearning for a home of his own—a place to hang his hat after a long day. It was a vision that looked a lot like the green pastures of Parma.

Napoleon's route of return was as meandering as his trip westward. Details are missing, but one can read between the lines when the

Napoleon Graham wandered for years before settling down at this prestigious farm in Parma Township. *From Everts & Stewart Combination Atlas Map of Jackson County, 1874.*

biographer states that the erstwhile explorer "returned home by way of the Isthmus of Panama and New York City. After this experience, Mr. Graham was content to settle down to farming pursuits, which he has since uninterruptedly followed."

He was so content, in fact, that he developed the 120-acre farm he inherited from his father into one of the premier farms of Parma Township. Census and other documents identify Napoleon B. Graham as a "farmer" who "erected substantial buildings" on the "well-tilled land." Finally, the wanderer had come home. He had gone from Panama to Parma to discover the proverbial pot of gold in his backyard.

In 1890, after developing a successful farm, this son of a restless Scot, onetime gold seeker and happy farmer, died at sixty-five years old. He was buried at Graham Cemetery in Parma.[43]

22

Pulaski Township

Fun Facts

- The area was first settled by Reuben Penogen and Matthias and Enoch Fisher, who came from Pennsylvania in 1833. The earliest permanent settler was John Howard, who located on what was subsequently called Howard's Island in 1834. Other early settlers included John Wilber; Colonel Luther L. Ward; Michael, Harvey and Harry Nowlin; and Isaac N. Swain.
- Pulaski Township was organized, combining parts of other townships, in 1837. Its present boundaries were determined in 1838. James Cross was the first supervisor. When Cross resigned six months later, Reverend J.B. Burroughs was elected supervisor.
- The original settlement of Pulaski was a mile west of the present community at the intersection of Folks and Watson Roads and was called Wheelerton. When the Cincinnati, Jackson and Mackinaw Railroad was built in 1884, several businesses clustered near the present location on Folks Road.
- Pulaski pioneer Colonel Ward named the town in honor of the Polish military commander Count Kazimierz Pulaski.[44]

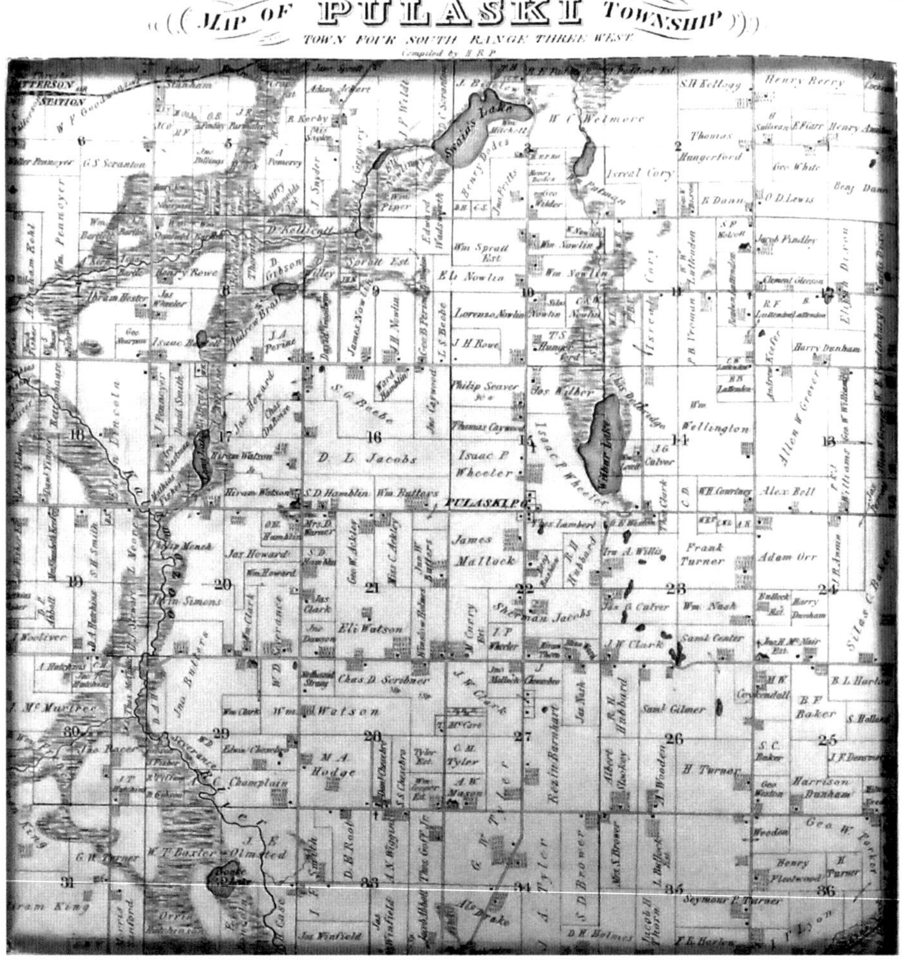

From Everts & Stewart Combination Atlas Map of Jackson County, 1874.

Neither Snow, Nor Rain…

Pulaski pioneer Isaac P. Wheeler (1817–1897) wore many hats as an early community leader. His biographer states Wheeler was "closely identified with almost every movement designed for the advancement of this township since its organization." Wheeler's list of accomplishments includes town clerk, supervisor, road commissioner and first local postmaster—a post he held for twenty years. In this capacity, he was responsible for "the first mail ever carried into Pulaski," a duty that seems minor compared to his other roles, but it was probably the most arduous.

Rural mail carriers in the early to mid-1800s were bold souls. They had to walk dozens of miles through a wilderness inhabited by wolves and bears in pouring rain, drifting snow and scorching heat. Roads were "poor at best, and nonexistent at worst." One of the early ads for the Pony Express hints at the potential dangers inherent in the mail carrier business with this comically blunt wording: "Wanted: Young, skinny, wiry fellows not over 18. Must be… willing to risk death daily. Orphans preferred."

In the discharge of his duties, Wheeler likely had to take the following oath required of all postmasters in 1860: "I ______, do swear/affirm that I will faithfully perform all the duties required of me, and abstain from everything forbidden by the laws in relation to the establishment of the Post Office and post roads within the United States." This motto could have applied to him as well: "Neither Rain, Nor Sleet, Nor Dark of Night Shall Stay These Couriers from the Swift Completion of Their Appointed Rounds."

Postmasters also had to keep the post office open during normal business hours and reside in the community where it was located. Generally, rural post offices were a sideline to the postmaster's primary occupation, such as storekeeper or, in Wheeler's case, farmer. He probably had help, but even

Father of the American Cavalry

Pulaski Township is named after Kazimierz Pulaski (1745–1779), a Polish nobleman and military commander often called the father of the American cavalry. Pulaski, who fought against Russian domination in his native land, traveled to America following a recommendation from American statesman Benjamin Franklin. Pulaski distinguished himself by becoming a general in the Continental army, reforming the American cavalry and saving the life of George Washington. He was killed during a daring charge against British forces.*

* "Kazimierz Pulaski," *Encyclopedia Britannica.*

so, the job would have kept the multitasker hopping, since mail volume grew roughly sixteen times faster than the U.S. population during the second half of the 1800s.

Wheeler performed his duties admirably, which also suggests that he was robust. His biographer stated, "All of Mr. Wheeler's efforts in life have been…crowned with success and, being possessed with a strong constitution, coupled with energy and thrift, bids fair to reach a higher round on the ladder of prosperity."

He did indeed become prosperous. His four-hundred-acre farm was so successful that it was depicted on an 1874 lithograph of prominent farms in Jackson County. In addition, he was likely the namesake for the settlement's original name, Wheelerton.

Censuses and other documents help flesh out other details about the life of this hardy pioneer. He was born to Loren and Eunice Wheeler in Middlesex County, Massachusetts, in 1817. His family migrated to Michigan in his youth. In adulthood, Wheeler spent about three years in Hillsdale County but found greener pastures in Pulaski Township, moving there around 1838. A biographer said Wheeler was part of Pulaski "since its organization." In 1841, he married Almira R. Wilbur. The couple had four children—three of their own and one by adoption.

The 1860 U.S. census indicates Wheeler was a forty-three-year-old farmer in Pulaski living with his forty-one-year-old wife, Almira; their three children;

Isaac P. Wheeler was a prominent Pulaski farmer and civic leader in the mid-1800s. *From Everts & Stewart Combination Atlas Map of Jackson County, 1874.*

and Almira's parents, Joseph and Lucy Wilbur. It must have been a close family. The 1880 census indicates Wheeler was a sixty-two-year-old widower whose eighty-year-old mother-in-law continued to live in his household. Almira died in 1877 and was buried at Pulaski Cemetery. In 1897, Isaac P. Wheeler was laid to rest beside his wife. His legacy, including the delivery of decades of letters and several civic roles, is part of Pulaski Township's lesser-known history.[45]

Isaac N. Swain: The Man Everyone Wanted

Swain's Lake County Park and Campground, operated by the Jackson County Parks system, is a popular spot for recreationists. The park offers fifty-six modern campsites, a twenty-six-acre campsite overlooking a lake, nature trails and a boat launch. As if that's not enough, the seventy-acre body of water in northern Pulaski Township is stocked with fish, and golf enthusiasts can enjoy an eighteen-hole course just across the street.

These benefits are clearly spelled out in county park literature. What's not clear is whether its namesake—Isaac N. Swain (1807–1880)—actually lived in Pulaski Township, since other townships have claimed him as well. Fortunately, there is more clarity about other aspects of this mover and shaker in Michigan.

Isaac N. Swain was born in Jefferson County, New York, to Martha and Richard Swain. His father's ancestors were among the earliest Quaker settlers in America, arriving from England in the late 1600s. Although Swain attended school in a log cabin, he had a "rare intelligence, cultivated by excessive reading," his biographer wrote. His family lived near a harbor, and young Swain had enough time to observe sailors under less-than-desirable conditions, which cultivated another passion—a hatred of intoxicating spirits.

At age fourteen, the industrious lad worked for the Erie Canal project and diligently saved his money. At sixteen, he was well read enough to get a teaching certificate and accepted positions throughout the South. On his return to the North, he made a prospecting tour into Michigan. He might have been searching for more than land. In 1830, he married Vallonia Smith of Detroit and made Michigan his permanent home.

Around 1831, the entrepreneur purchased land in Jackson and settled in what is now Spring Arbor with his wife and parents-in-law. Among his assets, Swain apparently also had a sense of humor, as was evident by the sign posted near his log cabin, which was roofed with hay. It read, "Swain's Hay Castle." In 1834, Swain moved near or to Swain's Lake. Boundaries were a bit vague during this period, since the lake was part of an enlarged Spring Arbor Township that also comprised present-day Concord, Hanover, Parma, Pulaski, Sandstone, Springport and Tompkins Townships.

To make matters even more confusing, Isaac N. Swain is specifically claimed as an early resident by Concord, Pulaski and Spring Arbor Townships in their histories. The book *Spring Arbor Township 1830–2013* affirms, however, that Swain did live on the lake he is named after, stating that he "owned property at the east end of Swain's Lake. He farmed, surveyed and ran a lumber mill." That would corroborate a much earlier historian who was less specific about the location of Swain's residence but conclusively stated that he was among Pulaski's early settlers.

Perhaps, in the end, everyone wanted to claim the man who was important enough to be included in the *American Biographical History of Eminent and Self-Made Men*. But Swain did not remain in Jackson. Disheartened at failed efforts to attract a canal or railroad to the area, in 1848, he moved to Watervliet, Michigan, where he operated a successful mill. This success was followed by loss a decade later, when Vallonia died. The next year, he married Eleanor Champion of Ypsilanti, sinking his roots even deeper into Michigan soil. During the Civil War, Swain was a staunch supporter of the Union cause. When the war ended, he moved to Detroit, where he made a small fortune in business. As an indication of his success, when he died in 1880, he left an estate worth $500,000.

Renowned businessman Isaac N. Swain, who once resided in Pulaski, was among Jackson's early movers and shakers. *Courtesy Spring Arbor University archives.*

His biographer portrayed Swain as a man who loomed larger than life, which might have been physically true as well, since he stood six feet, two inches tall. In comparison, the average man in the 1800s stood five feet, ten inches. His biographer wrote, "He is 6 feet 2 inches in height and is compactly built. He has a full, flowing beard, iron grey hair, light, clear complexion and a fine set of natural teeth….He is prompt, courteous and agreeable in all business transactions."

Isaac N. Swain, mover and shaker, Jackson pioneer and business tycoon, died in 1880. He is buried at Woodmere Cemetery in Detroit. All things considered, if a lake must be named after someone, Isaac Swain is an intriguing namesake.[46]

23
Rives Township

Fun Facts

- In 1834, Samuel Prescott built the first house in the township.
- Rives Township was organized into its present limits in 1837. The first meeting was held at the house of Oliver True, who lived in section 27, and the first supervisor was E.B. Chapman. Rives received its name from John C. Rives, an influential man in politics, who lived in Maryland when Andrew Jackson was president.
- Samuel Prescott became the first postmaster of the township in 1839. The office, established in his home, was called the West Rives Post Office.
- The first child born in the township was Sarah Prescott, daughter of Samuel Prescott.
- Rives is known as the "cornerstone" township because it is where Michigan's north/south (principle meridian) and east/west (base line) surveying lines intersect.
- The Rives Township website describes the township as "a community of farms and businesses bound together with generations of family ties and of neighbors working and living together."[47]

From Everts & Stewart Combination Atlas Map of Jackson County, 1874.

RIVES IRRESISTIBLE REAL ESTATE

John F. Drew (1828–1911) was determined to rise above the humble conditions of his birth. All he needed was the right setting. Drew, the son of a Scottish immigrant, was born on a farm in Shelby Basin, New York, in 1828. His education in the backwoods was "restricted," as his biographer delicately put it. But that didn't stop the dreamer from reaching for the stars.

His ticket to a better life, he determined, would be his father's livestock. Over the years, he observed animals' habits and developed an uncanny ability to bring out the best in his father's horses, cattle and hogs. His favorites, however, were sheep. He loved their soft wool and their gentle nature. Sheep, he decided, would get his full attention and would be the livestock on which he would stake his future. But first, he had to earn enough money to buy them.

As a young adult, Drew took various jobs, from cutting lumber to rafting commercial loads along the Erie Canal. By 1848, he had saved enough money to purchase a farm in New York and marry Elizabeth Baker. Eventually, he became civically and commercially active, serving as a justice of the peace and investing in the New York Stock Exchange. It turned out that Drew had a knack for the stock market, possibly involving livestock, and he became prosperous enough to buy herds of sheep. Over time, by careful breeding, he improved successive generations of the woolly creatures. But something was still missing—the farm location didn't feel right.

Around 1866, Drew read reports about Michigan's assets, and his dream started to come alive. As his biographer said, "Brief observation of the conditions in Michigan sufficed to convince him that at that particular time, farming could be made more profitable than any one particular line." After scouting out prospective land, the pastoral setting of Rives Township caught his eye. He was attracted to its rolling, lush landscape, and the price of land was irresistible. Finally, the stars aligned, and the setting was right. Later that year, Drew bought 120 acres in Rives Township, cleared the land and built a "fine residence and substantial buildings on the place."

In 1867, he and his wife moved into their new abode. Then he shipped the choicest of his sheep from New York to their new farm. To add icing to the cake, he purchased an exotic breed of sheep—Merino—known for its excellent wool quality with origins dating to twelfth-century Spain. His dream had finally come true—it was all waiting for him in Rives Township.

The result, as one historian put it, was favorable to Drew and beneficial to Michigan: "Much attention has been devoted to the improvement of live stock [*sic*] of various kinds…the number who have turned their attention to the improvement of sheep is not quite so great…and to…John F. Drew… much credit is due for the improvement of the latter in this section of the country." Drew's farm was so successful that it was included among sketches of prominent farms in an 1874 atlas map of Jackson County.

Over the years, Drew branched out into other arenas, serving as a justice of the peace and a state representative at various times. Even so, "the fascination he found in the care and observation of live stock [*sic*] could not be wholly suppressed."

Drew's contributions to farming and animal husbandry may be overlooked today, but he was one of many early Jacksonians whose success helped

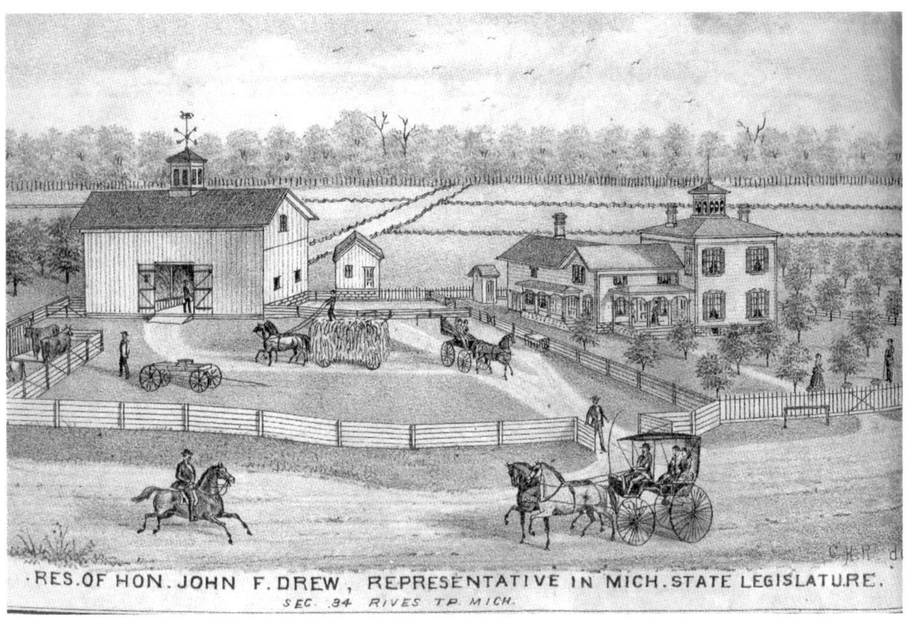

John F. Drew was a celebrated livestock farmer in Rives Township. *From Everts & Stewart Combination Atlas Map of Jackson County, 1874.*

propel Michigan's standing in the food and agriculture industry. John F. Drew, legislator, investor and sheep drover extraordinaire, died in 1911. He was buried in his beloved Rives Township at Jones Cemetery.[48]

THE CORNERSTONE TOWNSHIP

Every boundary line of historic significance in Michigan finds its source where Rives and Henrietta Townships intersect with Ingham County. That's because this intersection was the starting point of surveys that determined all the borders of every township in the state. The concept is similar to cutting a pie into similarly sized pieces. The carver must start from a central point. Rives Township was part of that point, which is why it's called the Cornerstone Township.

The history of this fascinating project goes back to 1815, when the government was tasked with dividing vast stretches of uncharted wilderness into territories and states. To accomplish this, surveyors were hired to

This circular metal marker in Rives Township memorializes one of two starting points for Michigan's boundaries. *Author's photo.*

establish a base line (east to west) and a principal meridian line (north to south). With these coordinates, all of the six-mile-square townships—and all of the thirty-six one-mile-square sections in them—could be established.

This delineation task may sound boring—like a giant math or science project spread out over land instead of paper. In reality, it was anything but boring. If the Rives Township soil could talk where the surveyors conducted their work, it would have tales to tell of hardship, surprise and iron-willed determination.

Audiences of such a time-bending story would hear about men venturing onto Rives's soil, carrying giant metal compasses, tripods, flags and heavy metal chains for measuring long distances. They would listen to tales of laborers encumbered with the supplies needed to survive for months in the wilderness, including food, clothing, bedding and gear. They would learn about outdoorsmen who were exposed to predators, heat and cold, hunger and thirst, diseases and accidents in unpopulated areas—men who had to travel across land where no roads existed. These weary workers had no cabin for shelter, only a soldier's tent. One surveyor wrote about the demands of his profession in this poignant reminiscence: "None but Men…always at home in Woods and Swamps [and who] can live upon what they afford, who can travel for Days up to their knees in mud and mire, can drink any fluid he finds while he is drenched with water also—and has a knowledge of the lands and who are equally patient and persevering under similar hardships can make anything by surveying the kind of Country we have to Survey."

Other surveyors wrote about axe men laboring to cut paths through impenetrable forests, flagmen sinking almost to their hips in mud and workers suffering through wet and cold with threadbare clothes, unable to buy anything warmer because no populated areas—or stores—were nearby. They did all this for the grand sum of two dollars per mile.

Their story is not one that made newspaper headlines, but perhaps it should have. Before any official settlements could appear in Michigan, before any residents could get legal title to any real estate, before the government knew anything about the land, surveying teams bravely crisscrossed every square mile of the state. Heading into uncharted wilderness and facing untold dangers, these intrepid workers ran lines that now determine every plot of land and every road in the state. And in Michigan, this vital undertaking began in Rives Township.[49]

MERIDIAN-BASELINE STATE PARK

The north to south Michigan meridian is 334 miles long, beginning at Fort Defiance, Ohio, and passing through Jackson on its way Sault Ste. Marie. The east to west baseline is 172 miles long and runs from Lake St. Clair to South Haven. The original survey had errors, so adjustments were made to later surveys, resulting in two points of reference and a baseline that crosses the meridian at those two points, about 936 feet apart. That's why Jackson County maps show a jog at the Rives-Henrietta Township border instead of a straight line. Surveyors refer to these twin points as the North and South Initial Points. Michigan is the only state to have such a "perturbation" in its public land survey. Both points are memorialized by metal cornerstones in Meridian-Baseline State Park, which straddles Jackson and Ingham Counties.

24
Sandstone Charter Township

Fun Facts

- Chester Wall was the first settler (1829), staking out property near Sandstone Creek. Samuel Roberts was the first pioneer to build a log cabin in the area (1830).
- James Valentine was the first postmaster in 1831.
- The village of Barry, which was platted in 1832, had hotels, stores, a church and other buildings. It was a rival of Jacksonburg until it was abandoned in the mid-1800s.
- The first teacher was Mary Parks in 1834.
- A super-sized Sandstone Township was organized in 1836, encompassing Sandstone, Parma, Springport and Tompkins Townships. John Barnum was elected supervisor. The present boundaries were established in 1839. Chester Wall was elected as supervisor. It received its name because of large deposits of sandstone rock along Sandstone Creek.[50]

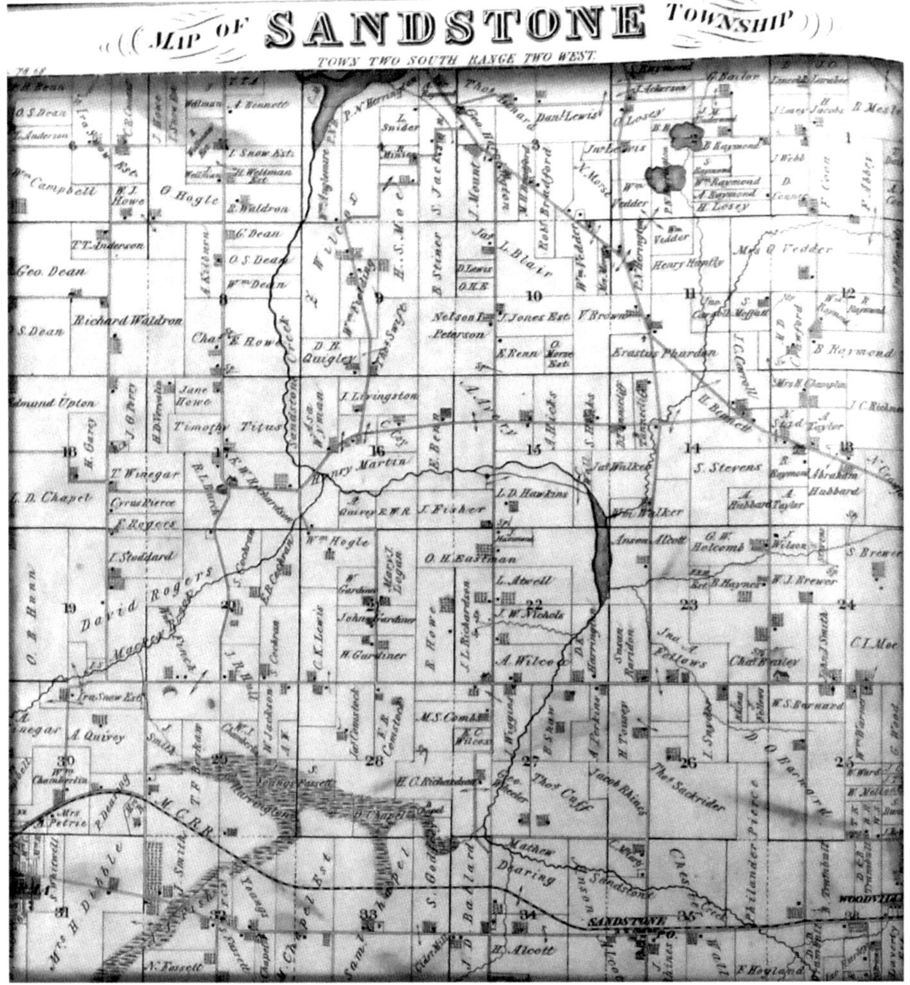

From Everts & Stewart Combination Atlas Map of Jackson County, 1874.

THE GHOST TOWN OF BARRY

Most townships have a ghost town or two, places where people once lived and worked but, over time, were deserted. Sandstone Township is no exception. In its borders is the phantom village of Barry, a once-thriving place that rivaled Jackson in commerce, prestige and potential. Over time, however, Barry went the way of all ghost towns, abandoned to all but memory—and perhaps ghosts. What happened to this town of great promise?

Barry's story begins with Samuel Roberts, a native New Yorker who moved to the area and settled along Sandstone Creek around 1830. The creek was named for large deposits of sandstone rock along its banks, providing valuable quarries later. Roberts liked the area enough to stay. Settlers followed soon afterward, creating momentum for future development.

The potential for even greater appeal occurred in 1832, when the Michigan territorial council passed an act calling for the organization of Jackson County. Left undecided were the choice of a new state capital and the selection of the county seat (town that is the governmental center of the county). Could Barry be a contender for both?

Enter entrepreneur Dr. D.K. Akers, who foresaw the marketability of the attractive, fertile land, as well as its profitability for himself as the developer. Between 1832 and 1834, Akers bought 160 acres of land near the intersection of Sandstone Road and West Michigan Avenue, filed a plat for a village and named it Barry, after William T. Barry, President Andrew Jackson's postmaster general from 1829 until 1835.

Akers moved aggressively to develop and sell the land, taking the plat to his hometown in Poughkeepsie, New York, and offering lots from twenty-five to one hundred dollars. The enterprising doctor also offered free medical care to all settlers for one year, among other inducements. Some who bought plats came to Michigan to settle in the new village, while others bought land on speculation. Akers spared no expense in developing his town. Between 1832 and 1835, he built a store, blacksmith shop, shoe shop, hotel and his large stone residence and nearby office, which doubled as a drugstore.

He also tended to settlers' spiritual needs, inducing Reverend Jason Park (also spelled "Parks"), a Presbyterian minister, to come to Barry and organize a church around 1833. One local historian recalled when people from Jackson would travel to Barry just to hear Reverend Park preach. Around 1835, Akers constructed a stone bank building, which, among other things, issued notes from the Farmer's Bank of Sandstone.

These were among the reasons Barry flourished and became not only a rival to Jacksonburg but also one of the most thriving communities in southern Michigan. It certainly vied as a contender for the county seat and possibly even the capitol. What could go wrong?

The end might have begun when the territorial council chose Lansing for the state capital and selected Jacksonburg—not Barry—as the county seat. The proverbial nail in the coffin, however, was hammered by the bank's willingness to circulate notes "far and wide without regard for whether there was sufficient funds to back them up."

Above: This building of sandstone slabs, once a thriving bank, is among remnants of the former village of Barry, Sandstone Township. *Author's photo.*

Left: The Congregational Church of Sandstone on South Sandstone Road worshipped in this building in 1872. *Courtesy Sandstone Congregational Church.*

In the early 1800s, banking regulation was minimal, and Farmer's Bank of Sandstone was one of the wildcat banks that went bust. Around 1838–39, the bank collapsed. Soon after this, as a historian said, "Barry receded in growth and importance, until it became simply a memory instead of an active fact."

Records could not be found that detailed what happened to the town's founder and eager promoter. A doctor with the initials or surname of "D.K. Akers" once living in Jackson County or Poughkeepsie, New York, does not show up in any U.S. census count in Michigan. The pastor he recruited, however, remained in Jackson, tending to his farm, rearing his daughters and pastoring the church until he died in 1849. Reverend Jason Park is buried at Dearing Cemetery in Sandstone.

Likewise, the church, which was organized in 1834, continues to this day as the Sandstone Congregational Church. It has undergone several transitions from a log house to a frame house dedicated in 1872 to the new church complex built immediately south of the original building in 2004. There is one other remnant in this ghost town: the original stone bank, which might have collapsed financially but still stands structurally. These two buildings, the enduring church and the empty bank, are all that is left of the phantom village of Barry.[51]

JANE BENN: FROM PIONEER WIFE TO FARM ADMINISTRATOR

If Jane Benn's (1835–1916) only legacy was survival, it would be enough. This Sandstone Township pioneer was predeceased by four children, her husband, her parents and her parents-in-law. But survival is not her only legacy. Jane left a life of ease to marry a backcountry woodsman, bear ten children, oversee considerable property while a widow and retain enough grace through it all to be highly regarded by her neighbors. She was also among few women included in a biography of notable Jacksonians.

Jane was born in Toronto, Canada, the only daughter of Irish immigrants James and Jane Barber. The couple also had one son, Joseph, who was two years younger. The patriarch, who received "limited educational advantages" in his youth, "endeavored to bestow greater privileges upon his offspring," so he moved his family to Ann Arbor.

Working as a successful gardener and serving as a postmaster in Ann Arbor, James had the wherewithal to enroll Jane in "Mrs. Eliza Page's seminary." Apparently, Jane was a top student because she graduated "quite young, at 14 years old," said her biographer, adding that Jane was a "cultured and refined woman." After school, Jane learned the tailoring trade, which she successfully pursued for three years.

James's reaction when Jane married Elijah Benn was not recorded. But one can only imagine the father's response when his educated only daughter was united in marriage with a backcountry woodsman, whose home was a log shanty in the woods. The couple settled on section 16 of Sandstone Township. Their biographer stated that the couple "began their married life in the wilderness from which they hewed out a home....Elijah was a woodsman who chopped all the timber that was cut on the place and was noted as the best wood chopper in the neighborhood."

Jane "devoted herself with all the energy of her nature to the welfare of her husband and children, not neglecting deeds of neighborly kindness." The losses encountered by this steadfast woman began around 1863, when her brother, who served in Company G, Tenth Michigan Infantry, died in Atlanta, Georgia, during the Civil War. Her father died shortly thereafter, "hastened by the loss of his only son." Over the next several years, five more

Jane Benn efficiently managed this extensive Sandstone Township farm after her husband died. *From Everts & Stewart Combination Atlas Map of Jackson County, 1874.*

family members died: Jane's four children and her beloved husband, Elijah, in 1884. Both of her parents-in-law had also passed away.

By that time, Elijah, "whose honesty and uprightness were well-known," had accumulated 120 acres of land in addition to a home, a large barn and several other buildings. It was a lot to run for the widow, but Jane was up to the task. According to her biographer, Jane possessed "good business qualifications," "wisely" managed the affairs that had been left in her hands and was "highly respected by all."

In 1900, Jane continued to live alone on her Sandstone Township farm, according to the U.S. census of that year, which also showed that she was a widow who could read and write. By 1910, however, her son Elijah had moved to the farm and was living with her. In 1916, this eighty-one-year-old daughter of Irish immigrants who left a life of ease to share the burdens of pioneer life with her husband—this survivor whose rise to prominence was marked by grace and goodwill—died. She was buried at Pherdun Cemetery in Sandstone Township.[52]

25

Spring Arbor Township

Fun Facts

- Spring Arbor Township—the township of many springs—once held a large Potawatomi encampment, including burial sites and council grounds in its southwestern portion.
- Benjamin Packard was among the first settlers in the township, buying land in section 29 in 1831. He occupied the land with his family in 1835. Other early settlers included A.B. Gibson, Moses Bean and William Smith and his son-in-law, Isaac Newton Swain, who bought 480 acres from 1831 until 1833.
- Spring Arbor Township's boundaries underwent several changes, from a supersized township in 1833 to the current boundaries established in 1838.
- The original 128-acre Spring Arbor village, platted by Packard and Swain in 1835, was located near Hammond and Cross Roads.
- The institution known today as Spring Arbor University underwent several transformations and location changes from 1835, when the Michigan Legislative Council granted a charter for the Spring Arbor School, to 1873, when the property was purchased by the Free Methodists and became Spring Arbor Seminary, the predecessor of today's university.
- Spring Arbor was selected by Businessweek.com among communities listed as Best Small Town to Raise Children in 2011.[53]

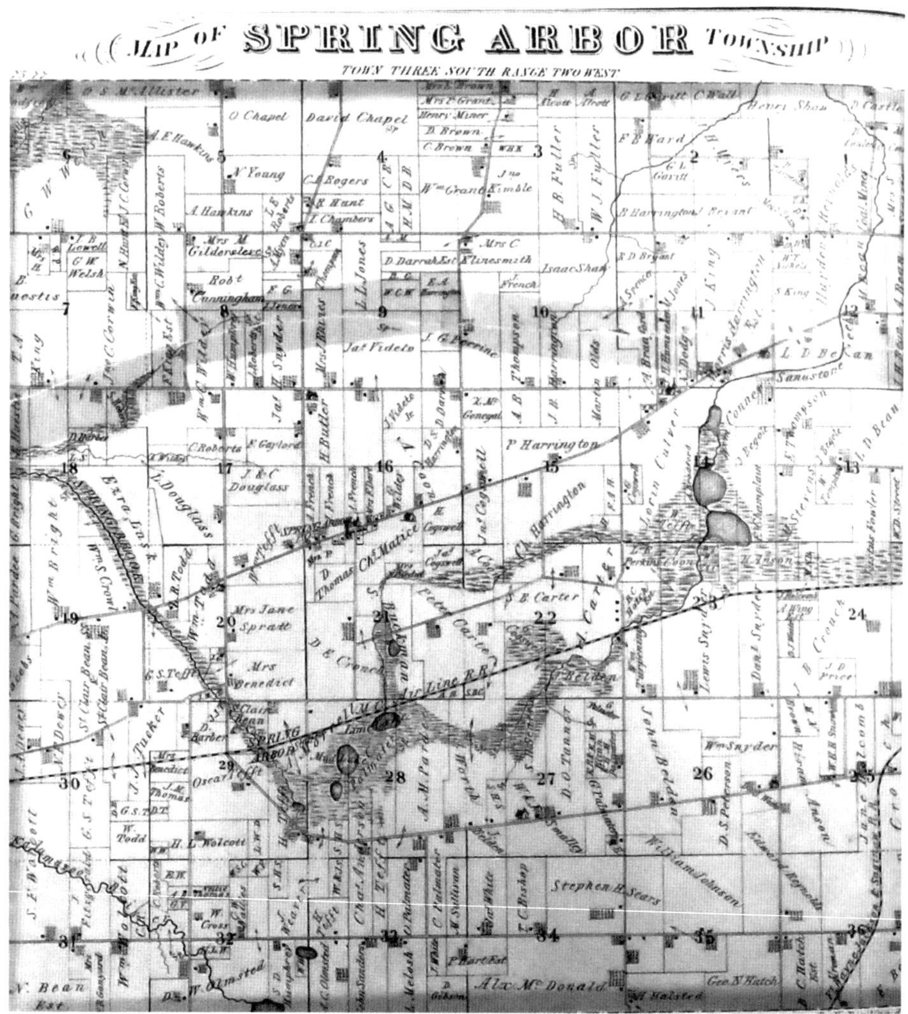

From Everts & Stewart Combination Atlas Map of Jackson County, 1874.

THE DEEP ROOTS OF SPRING ARBOR FREE METHODIST CHURCH

If someone predicted that you would follow a rebel preacher from England, that your decision would attract dozens of like-minded souls and that the church building and congregation would become the largest of its kind in the nation, would you believe it? The founders of today's Spring Arbor Free

Methodist Church may not have foreseen that outcome, but it happened that way, just the same.

The roots of the church at 120 East Main Street date to 1738, when a young Anglican preacher named John Wesley ventured outside the safety of his local pulpit in England to take God's message of love, grace and salvation to common people throughout the island nation. Wesley, considered a rebel by the establishment, called believers to holiness in personal and social life and traveled far and wide on horseback to preach in settings that ranged from cornfields to coal mines. His efforts launched a grassroots revival in England and beyond, eventually spreading to the newly organized colonies in America.

The resulting Methodist Church in America was organized in 1785 and grew rapidly. Over time, however, differences of opinion began dividing various groups. By the mid-1800s, some strongly objected to slavery, pew rentals and secret societies, among other differences. Others did not.

In 1857, Benjamin Titus Roberts, a young Methodist Episcopal preacher from Buffalo, New York, protested what he saw as the departure from the principles of early Wesleyan doctrine. He published a pamphlet called *New School Methodism* that critiqued these practices. The publication unleashed a firestorm of controversy, ultimately leading to the expulsion of Roberts and other sympathizers, beginning in 1858. Although few could know it at the time, the waves created by this expelled preacher were about to ripple across the nation and crest in the small township of Spring Arbor.

Many Methodist pastors had read Roberts's pamphlet and were impressed, including one from Missouri, who invited Roberts to meet with his congregation and organize it as an independent church. Roberts accepted the invitation, but when he arrived in Missouri, he was appalled at the prevalence of slavery. He voiced his objections, prompting considerable debate in the church, but the congregation ultimately aligned with Roberts's antislavery position. It was a sign of things to come.

The fledgling group chose the name Free Methodist to reflect its beliefs that slavery is opposed to scripture, church pews must be free for all, secret societies conflict with Christian freedom and freedom of expression includes freedom in the Holy Spirit. Members also strongly believed that freedom and simplicity of worship should include all people, regardless of racial, economic or social standing. These tenets, members believed, best reflected John Wesley's values.

The Free Methodist Church was formally organized in 1860 in Pekin, New York, and began spreading across the country. Around 1870, a Free

In the 1920s, the Spring Arbor Free Methodist Church met in this stone building, which has since been demolished. *Courtesy, Spring Arbor University archives.*

Methodist pastor named Edwin Payson Hart organized several churches throughout southern Michigan. This led to the establishment of a small congregation in the Spring Arbor area during the winter of 1870–71. The congregation's first house of worship was a stone schoolhouse near the corner of Mathews Road and M-60. A new brand of Methodism had come all the way from England to find a welcome home in Spring Arbor.

In 1873, the congregation bought property on the campus of the former Free Will Baptist School (today the campus of Spring Arbor University.) As the congregation grew, members held services in various locations, including another stone church it built in 1922 on the corner of Cottage and Main Streets.

In 1963, it constructed a new building with a 700-seat sanctuary and other rooms. The building was expanded in stages and now includes a 1,600-seat sanctuary, a gymnasium, a kitchen, offices, fellowship rooms and classrooms. Roberts's vision of a church body challenged to live out its faith, meet together in a worshipful community and go into the world to preach the gospel has blossomed in ways that might have surprised even him.

Today, the Spring Arbor Free Methodist Church is the largest church in its denomination in the nation. Over the years, it has trained hundreds of pastors and lay leaders, birthed other congregations and funded missionaries locally and around the world. That's quite a legacy for a small group that was so inspired by a rebel preacher from England that it began meeting in a one-room schoolhouse in Spring Arbor Township.[54]

Amasa M. Pardee: Farmer, Civic Leader, Devout Pioneer

Amasa M. Pardee (1826–1901) was known for many admirable qualities. The longtime Spring Arbor resident was a loyal friend to Native Americans, a talented singer and a hardworking farmer. But the trait his descendants most remember was his devout faith.

According to his grandson, the patriarch "rarely departed" from his morning ritual of prayer and Bible reading, unless the day was "particularly conducive to farming." Under these favorable conditions, Amasa reasoned that the Almighty would understand if prayers were omitted, as long as a "double session" was held the next day. Amasa also led the Methodist Episcopal church choir, sang at funerals, and even preached the sermon if the minister was absent.

The pious pioneer came to Spring Arbor as a five-year-old with his family in 1832. The Pardees were from hardy stock. Amasa's father and grandfather walked from Detroit to Spring Arbor to select desirable tracts of land in 1831 and then the two men walked to the land offices at White Pigeon in southern Michigan, following marked trees on Indian trails. At night, they built campfires and slept on the ground. The total distance the Pardee men walked for this real estate venture was 220 miles—and that didn't include the trip back to Detroit, which was presumably on foot as well.

After returning to their native New York, the families collected their belongings and moved to Spring Arbor in 1832. Amasa's father, Thomas; his mother, Eleanore; and their children, including Amasa, settled on section 27. There, Thomas built a shanty, followed by a more substantial log cabin later. Amasa recalled that the "nearest neighbor was five miles away." The local Native Americans, who were "numerous but peaceful," became "greatly attached to the family." In fact, Thomas frequently "went to sleep with six or eight (braves) lying around the fire rolled up in their blankets."

Amasa M. Pardee, a successful farmer in Spring Arbor Township, was a devout Christian. *From Everts & Stewart Combination Atlas Map of Jackson County, 1874.*

When Eleanore peered out the window at the sleeping figures silhouetted by the flickering campfire, she "petitioned heaven to protect her loved ones." Then, to hedge her bets, she "slept with one eye open," Amasa recalled.

The lad was put to work on the farm at an early age, driving an ox team to help clear the land, but he also found time for studies. In adulthood, Amasa attended Michigan Central College in Spring Arbor, and he taught in the district school for several years. By 1845, he had saved enough money to buy 320 acres of land in Spring Arbor Township. After selling off some land in later years, he retained 206 acres.

In 1850, Amasa married Julia LaDue of Concord. The couple had three children. In 1852, he was made inspector of schools. He then served in a series of civic roles, including township supervisor, town clerk and justice of the peace. In addition to all of this, he found time to manage his farm, all of which was cultivated, enclosed with fences and supplied with "neat and substantial buildings." Among his specialties were "good grades of cattle and swine."

In 1910, the strong voice of Amasa was stilled. This hardworking farmer, friend of Native Americans and devout Christian was laid to rest at Spring Arbor Cemetery. Amasa was not the kind of resident who made the headlines. He didn't cure cancer, make a million dollars or perform on stage. But he is exactly the kind of person who contributed to Jackson County's growth and development in countless uncelebrated ways. Amasa Pardee is among the everyday heroes of Jackson County.[55]

26

Springport Township

Fun Facts

- Ebenezer Brown was among the first settlers in 1834, locating on what was later known as the Landon Farm (named after subsequent owners). Other early settlers included John S. Comstock, John Oyer, Edward and Augustus Ferris and O.V. Hammond.
- John Comstock built the first barn in 1835 and broke sod on the first piece of land.
- Springport Village was largely developed by John Oyer, who helped build the first store, hotel, mill and more. For many years, the town was known as Oyer's Corners. The village was incorporated in 1882.
- The first schools were taught by Julia Mallory and Luther Ludlow. The first frame schoolhouse was built in 1838.
- Springport Township was organized in 1838. Josiah Whitman was the first supervisor. The name "Springport" was coined by Augustus Ferris, who suggested it in honor of a New York town known for its many springs.[56]

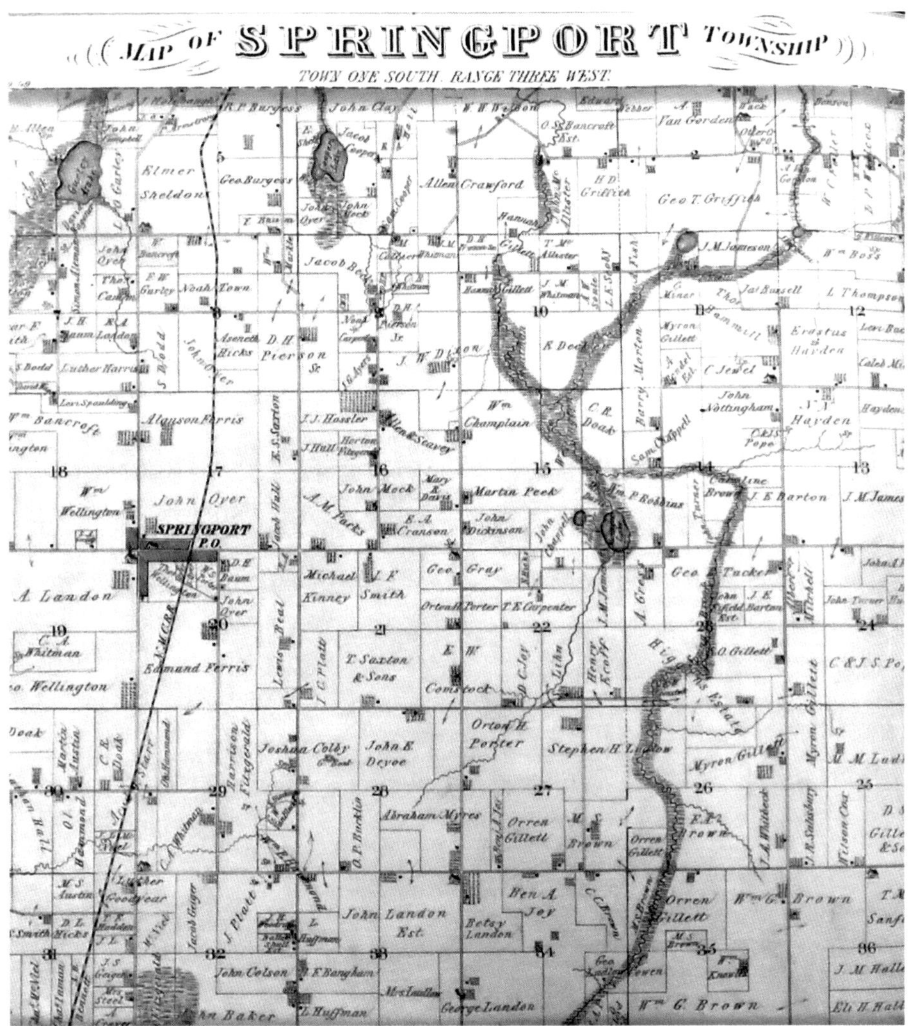

From Everts & Stewart Combination Atlas Map of Jackson County, 1874.

High Hopes

"High Hopes," a 1959 hit song, describes the challenge faced by an ant that wants to bring down a rubber tree plant—a seemingly impossible task since rubber tree plants are notoriously difficult to uproot. But the unyielding ant ignores critics who call his goals "pie in the sky," and ultimately prevails.

Daniel Griffith (1793–1867) and his family faced a similar challenge when they moved to Springport Township in 1835. Daniel's goal of deforesting over one hundred acres seemed improbable, but he tackled the task with grit and determination. While he didn't remove any rubber tree plants, he did uproot enough trees to turn the acreage into one of the premier farms of Jackson County. What it took to achieve that outcome provides a fascinating glimpse of the trials and triumphs of pioneer farming.

The first obstacle the family faced when they arrived in section 2 was lack of space for their dwelling. Their property was "in the midst of the virgin forest," so Daniel and his sons had to first clear a patch of land to have enough open space to build a log cabin. Deer, bears and wolves were plentiful, so members always kept their trusty rifles nearby.

With a roof over their heads, Daniel, his wife, Harriet, and their five sons turned their attention to farming. Fortunately, the family owned horses and oxen—the only such livestock in the township at the time. But even horsepower did not eliminate the problems of maneuvering around the rocks and stumps on their land, making plowing more like navigating a minefield. Son George Griffith recalled how the men had to guide "the slow-moving and dejected ox team before the plow, in addition to felling trees, splitting

Daniel and Betsy Griffith owned one of the premier farms of Springport Township. *From Everts & Stewart Combination Atlas Map of Jackson County, 1874.*

The Griffith farm was one of the largest in Springport Township. *From Everts & Stewart Combination Atlas Map of Jackson County, 1874.*

rails, chopping wood and fulfilling the manifold other functions which fell to the lot of the pioneer."

Buying supplies was not much easier. Early on, obtaining flour and other provisions for the farm required a 200-mile round-trip to Detroit via horse-drawn wagon. Selling their first crop of wheat was slightly easier, since it required a mere 120-mile round-trip to Ann Arbor. Daniel supplemented his farming income by serving as postmaster from the time the post office opened on his property in 1839 until he died almost three decades later. The office was known as Otter Creek.

Harriet was described as an "able helper" in the labors and struggles of pioneer life, "spinning and weaving both wool and flax and making clothing for the entire family." But life was hard, and she died in 1847, at the age of forty-eight. Sometime before 1850, Daniel married Betsy L.

By 1860, Springport had its own merchants, much to the relief of the travel-weary residents. The first store, owned by John Oyer, initially stocked a barrel each of flour and sugar, fifteen pounds of coffee, two pounds of tea, some tapioca, sodium carbonate, a few yards of calico and six spools of thread, among other popular supplies.

By this time, Daniel, who had acquired 240 acres of cultivated land, could afford to buy whatever supplies the family needed. Indeed, this "ant" had not only felled the proverbial rubber tree plant, but he had also transformed the soil into profitable yields and added livestock to his farm, including cattle, sheep, swine and horses.

At the end of his life, Daniel could look back on his "many days of toil and endeavor" with satisfaction. The labors of this determined "ant" resulted in "one of the most attractive rural domains in the country." Daniel Griffith, the farmer unafraid to dream big, died in 1867. He was laid to rest at Griffith Cemetery in Springport at the age of seventy-four.[57]

CIVIL WAR REMINISCENCES

It's easy to reduce the Civil War to a series of battles, facts and figures when viewed from a national perspective. Seen from a local perspective, however, the personal impact of this bloody war becomes more real and more palpable. Springport is among localities that can provide this intimate perspective, thanks to the archival efforts of its residents, beginning with a firsthand description of how inhabitants first reacted to the conflict on April 12, 1861.

"The news of the firing on Fort Sumpter [*sic*] was first brought to Springport by a man named Rogers, who came…from Parma on foot," wrote Ben A. Joy in his book *Pioneer History of Springport Township*. Joy, who was born before the Civil War and lived through it, wrote from personal experience and included the personal stories of returning veterans and their relatives in a chapter titled "War Reminiscences."

Joy recalled that the declaration of war caused a collective "shudder to pass over the people," followed by a "quiet determination to stand by the old flag." He also recounted residents' naive expectations of the war's duration: "three months' service…was thought by many to be a sufficient time to quell the rebellion and maintain the government." In reality, the War Between the States lasted four bloody years and took the lives of about 620,000 in the North and South, not counting postwar survivors who died from suicide, posttraumatic stress and other causes.

Joy's reminiscences, published by the *Springport Signal* in 1910, range from the sad to the comical, including the three local lads who wanted to enlist but always seemed to be a step behind. Since Springport had no railroad in 1861, the three men had to trudge from Springport to Jackson to enlist. When they arrived, they discovered their group, Company E, First Michigan, had just left Jackson for Washington, D.C., so they "immediately followed after," presumably not on foot.

The weary trio caught up with the Michigan regiment near Manassas, Virginia, just in time to jump into the First Battle of Bull Run, the first major

The poignant memoirs of many Civil War veterans are preserved in the book *Pioneer History of Springport Township*. *Author's photo, Jackson Civil War Muster.*

fighting of the Civil War and a complete Confederate victory. But the men persevered, and when their time of enlistment expired, they reenlisted in the Twelfth Regular, where one ultimately lost his life and was "buried beneath the soil of the sunny south." The other two were honorably discharged at the war's close.

In another section, Joy recounts a somewhat humorous exchange between a Union sergeant commanding a boat and a civilian dock worker in New Orleans, Louisiana. When the boat approached the harbor, a rope was thrown at a dock worker so that he could fasten the boat to the dock. Instead, the dock worker defiantly let the rope fall into the water. With time

Catching Jefferson Davis

James Bert Judson (1844–1911) enlisted in Company D, Michigan Fourth Cavalry Regiment in 1862. He was among men from the Fourth Michigan who, in 1865, captured Jefferson Davis, president of the Confederate States of America. He received $300 in prize money for his part in the capture. Judson, who went on to become a doctor in Springport, died in 1911. He was buried at Springport Cemetery.

running out, the Union sergeant reeled the rope back onto the boat and threw it again, but this time, he drew his gun and ordered the worker to catch the rope. The next line in the account simply states that the dock man "immediately complied with the order."

Readers can sense the fragility of life throughout this bloody war in several recollections, including the description of the battle at Petersburg, Virginia, where Springport resident Charles E. Pickett was shot in the left arm and began bleeding profusely. His comrade, Charles Scoby, tried to wrap the wound "to keep him [Pickett] from bleeding to death" but was shot and killed in the process.

Among the more interesting stories was that of Springport resident James B. Judson, who participated in many battles and campaigns, including the capture of Jefferson Davis, the president of the Confederate States of America. The capture took place near Irwinsville, Georgia, on May 10, 1865, for which Judson received a reward, along with the other men in his group.

Joy's pride in the township's patriotism is evident throughout the book and is perhaps best summed up by his assertion that whenever the government issued a call for more men, "Springport's quota was promptly filled, as was every subsequent call."[58]

27

Summit Township

Fun Facts

- Summit Township was organized in 1857. According to a local historian, Summit's "early history is closely interwoven with that of Jackson, as one half of the area of the city was taken out of its limits."
- Early settlers (not in the city) included Chester Bennett, L.G. Perry, Leander McCain, Jacob Hutchins and Ami Filley, to name a few.
- Summit Township contains land that is among the highest elevations in the county.
- The Grand River runs through the township, feeding many lakes as it courses through the county on to Lake Michigan.
- A historian noted that the value of Summit's territory "is shown by the fact that its 19,000 acres have been equalized for years as the highest of any farming lands in the county."[59]

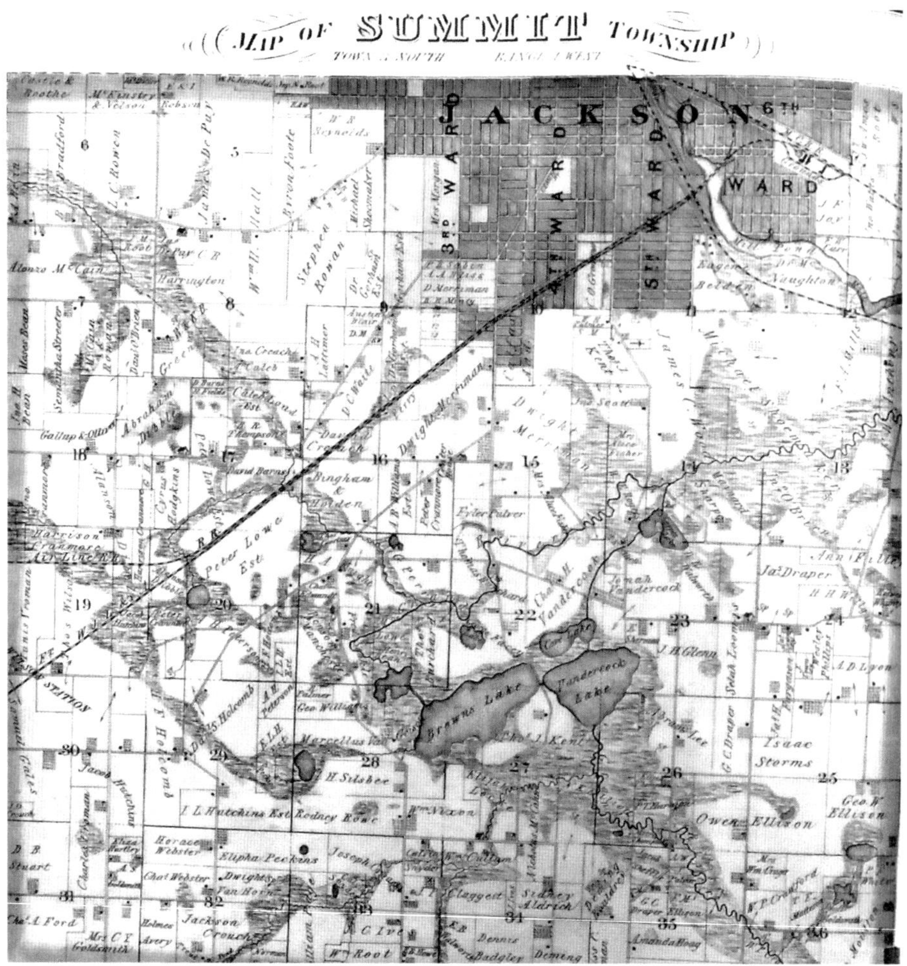

From Everts & Stewart Combination Atlas Map of Jackson County, 1874.

THE FIRST LADY OF BROWN'S LAKE

Brown's Lake residents have always thought of their lake as a hidden gem nestled in a peaceful patch of green. The private body of water in Summit Township exudes a quiet, inviting ambiance that has long attracted those seeking a reprieve from the hustle and bustle.

But on a cool autumn day in 1935, this quiet lake community was thrown into a tizzy when it hosted the first lady of the land. Lake neighbors weren't the only ones to react. The press went apoplectic, straining to get a glimpse of her person in spite of blocked roads and bodyguards. What happened next is the stuff of lore, except a long-forgotten newspaper article testifies that it was true.

The excitement began on the calm morning of Monday, September 9, 1935. Eleanor Roosevelt arrived at a Grass Lake train depot en route to join her brother G. Hall Roosevelt for a quiet, secluded siesta at a Brown's Lake cottage, owned by Howard Marsh of Jackson. The plan was for Mrs. Roosevelt to take a break from the paparazzi and enjoy a leisurely stroll along a secluded shore before attending an engagement in Detroit. Ah, the beauty of nature; ah, the fresh air; ah, the curiosity of neighbors with binoculars.

After being greeted at the Grass Lake train station by a contingent of state police officers in plain clothes, Mrs. Roosevelt was escorted to the secluded Summit Township cottage. As a safety precaution, Captain William Hanson and his men shut off the only road leading to the cottage. No reporters were to be admitted.

In an ideal world, that outcome might have transpired, but this was not an ideal situation. Brown's Lake is a tight-knit community that wanted to know what the fuss was all about and why one of the roads was blocked. News of Mrs. Roosevelt's whereabouts traveled fast among neighbors, proving that the old-fashioned grape vine was faster than greased lightning.

The peaceful ambiance of Brown's Lake once attracted First Lady Eleanor Roosevelt to the private lake in Summit Township. *Courtesy Jackson District Library.*

As the newspaper article stated, "It wasn't long before they [neighbors] were able, without the aid of field glasses, which, however, would have been used if necessary, to discover the wife of the president and her brother... apparently having a dandy time along the lake shore. The whispered news was passed along to reporters."

Once reporters arrived, the cat was out of the bag and the world learned another shocking secret: the first lady's attire was, well, "unconventional." As the reporter said, "It may be that this reporter is violating a confidence in telling the world that Mrs. Roosevelt wore shorts. He wasn't supposed to see her or know that her garb was 'unconventional.'"

The article added that a reporter who attempted to "sneak" through the woods was promptly turned back by Captain Hanson's men. Nevertheless, one reporter was able to not only sneak a peek at the unconventionally attired first lady, but he also snapped a photo later in the day, which just happened to make the front page of the *Jackson Citizen Patriot*.

Now, Mrs. Roosevelt was no dummy. She knew when she was spied on. But she also had a reputation for graciousness. When it was time for her to leave for Detroit, where she was dedicating a slum clearance project, the first lady went to the fridge to take stock of the provisions at hand. Making the best of the limited choices, she took it upon herself to make cheese and tomato sandwiches for the entire press, who peered from behind trees and strained from a distance.

Her act of kindness drew out the voyeurs like moths to a candle as they heartily partook of her offering. Among other privileged people to see her were a gardener, milkman, grocery delivery boy and unidentified guest.

Was Mrs. Roosevelt irritated at how this unwanted intrusion interrupted her day? Did she lose her gracious spirit? Reporters heard her exclaim, as she drove out of sight, her deep appreciation for the invitation and a wish to end urban blight.

So ends the true tale of Brown's Lake's first lady.[60]

The Glory Days of Hague Park

The glory days of Hague Park are long gone, but a cement pad on what is now Vandercook Lake Park bears silent witness that the spot was more than just a bathing/picnic area and boat launch at one time. In the early 1900s, it was a social magnet that drew thousands of people to a host of dazzling attractions.

The allure of the spot began humbly. In the 1890s, it was a picnic area developed by farmer Edrick Hague on land he owned near the east side of Vandercook Lake. Before long, the appeal of the location caught the attention of entrepreneurs who saw its potential. They leased 110 acres from Hague and turned it into an amusement park, which they named after the former owner. One of the financiers, James O'Dell, moved to Jackson to manage the development.

In 1907, Hague sold the property outright to O'Dell, who held nothing back in its development. The eager entrepreneur added a vaudeville theater, a high slide into the water (at thirty-five cents per hour), a bowling alley, a roller-staking rink, a fish pond, a merry-go-round, a steamboat that offered rides around the lake, concession stands, shooting galleries, balloon ascensions and fireworks on the Fourth of July. The unquestioned star of the park, however, was the Jack Rabbit, a roller coaster that took passengers straight up about fifty feet and then plunged downward—all for five cents per ride.

Originally, horse-drawn trolleys transported visitors from the city to the park and back, but with the advent of electricity, streetcars were added at five cents a ride. The cars funneled a steady stream of hot, weary city dwellers to the amusement park, which offered refreshing breezes off the

Hague Park on Vandercook Lake was a summer hot spot in Summit Township in the early 1900s. *Courtesy Jackson District Library.*

Jack Rabbit, a roller coaster, was the most popular amusement in Hague Park, Summit Township. *Courtesy Jackson District Library.*

lake, scenic views and enticing attractions. The July 5, 1912 issue of the *Jackson Citizen Patriot* reflected the park's draw. The article, titled "Immense Crowd at Hague Park," states, "Conservative estimates of the attendance…place the number at 30,000….A total of twenty-three [street]cars were in operation on the resort line and they were crowded to the platforms and running boards….Dancing, boating and bathing afforded pleasure for many holiday celebrators while everyone enjoyed the music furnished by the Boos Band…the [Fourth of July] fireworks were very elaborate."

The park's decline began in 1923, when a fire rendered its pump house, the first line of defense against fires, useless. Complicating matters, Jackson firefighters couldn't help because the city fire commission prohibited the department from fighting fires outside city limits. The blaze destroyed seven buildings in less than an hour. Making matters worse, insurance that could have covered the loss had expired six months prior. Arson was suspected but never proven. The rides and concessions continued, but the park's appeal began to decline.

In 1926, the father and son team of Eugene and Edmund Bethel from Columbus, Ohio, bought the park, made some improvements and changed its name to Lakeview Park. Any headway gained by enhancements was lost in 1929, when the Great Depression struck, and residents lacked cash for leisure events. Ultimately, the park fell into disrepair and was abandoned until 1938, when the land became a county park.

Today, visitors to Vandercook Lake Park still have much to see and do, from swimming, fishing and boating to renting kayaks at a livery. But the glory days of Hague Park have faded into the night like sunsets over the lake. Only memories ride the roller coaster's invisible tracks these days. All that's left of the amusement park is the cement pad that stood at the base of Jack the Rabbit. If only cement could talk, that slab would have quite an exciting story to tell.[61]

THE EXOTIC INSPIRATION FOR THE CASCADES

To most Jacksonians, the illuminated man-made waterfall known as the Cascades is as all-American as baseball and apple pie. After all, its creator, William "Cap" Sparks (1873–1943), was president of the Boy Scouts, a longtime Jackson resident and three-time mayor.

His dream was to create an enduring tourist destination in Jackson, and Sparks, a wealthy industrialist, had the wherewithal to make it happen. The result was the Cascades (also known as the Cascade Falls), a Summit Township landmark comprising sixteen concrete falls, multiple pools and majestic fountains. The attraction, which opened in 1932, rises sixty-four feet, extends five hundred feet down the side of a hill and is illuminated by 1,230 lights that form vibrant colors that are choreographed to music.

The waterfall, under the management of the Jackson County Parks Department, has undergone several repairs and renovations over the years, but it remains one of Jackson's most famous attractions. It's also a hot spot for picnicking families, summer festivals and sunset spectating—hallmarks of an all-American experience.

But the truth behind the landmark's inspiration is a bit more exotic. This man-made wonder finds its inspiration in Barcelona, Spain. Sparks, best known for forming the world-famous Withington Zouaves drill team, was so impressed with fountains he saw in Barcelona while touring with the Zouaves that he wanted to replicate the spectacle in his hometown.

He never identified which Spanish fountain inspired him, but there are several in Montjuic, Barcelona, Spain, including the Plaça de les Cascades, which features multiple pools flowing into one another, lighted fountains and square planter boxes. The Spanish fountains existed as early as 1929—the

The Cascades, an illuminated man-made waterfall and tourist attraction in Summit Township, was likely inspired by fountains in Spain. *Courtesy Jackson District Library.*

timeframe in which Sparks was traveling. Is Jackson's waterfall nothing more than a European imitation? Not exactly. The Barcelona fountains are in the middle of a city surrounded by traffic, and the Jackson waterfall is nestled in a county park filled with picnic tables and walking trails. What could be more American than that?[62]

28

Tompkins Township

Fun Facts

- The first settlers were Nicholas Townley and his sons, who bought land in sections 19 and 30 in the early 1830s and built the first log house. Other early settlers included Gardner G. Gould, David Adams, Joseph Wade and James Davenport.
- Tompkins Township was organized in 1838. At this meeting, Nicholas Townley was elected supervisor.
- Settlers originally wanted to name the township in honor of a respected resident, David Adams, who built the first barn in the township.
- The name of the township was proposed by Robert Anderson, who was an admirer of David D. Tompkins, a New York governor best known for spending his own money to equip the militia during the War of 1812.
- The first school was taught by Mary Hulburt in a small log house on land owned by James Davenport.[63]

From Everts & Stewart Combination Atlas Map of Jackson County, 1874.

HOME ALONE: SURVIVAL VERSION

In the popular movie *Home Alone*, a youngster fends off intruders while alone in a spacious house filled with modern conveniences. Edward Townley experienced the pioneer survival version of that scenario for seven months in the 1830s, but his home was a log cabin in the middle of the wilderness, and his intruders weren't people but wild beasts.

Edward's story began when he and his father, Nicholas Townley, left the family farm in New York to investigate land prospects in the Michigan Territory. The duo made the 480-mile trip with a horse-drawn wagon in

June. When Nicholas ventured into the Tompkins area, he liked what he saw—fertile land and abundant timber. He promptly bought 240 acres in sections 19 and 30. Then he and Edward began chopping trees and building a thirty-foot-by-thirty-six-foot log cabin for the family of nine—a mansion compared to most smaller dwellings.

The project took a little longer than Nicholas had expected, and he didn't depart for New York, where the rest of his family was waiting, until late September. Rather than leave the new house unoccupied for squatters, Nicholas decided to leave Edward behind to safeguard their investment. Nicholas's plan was to return with the rest of the family before it got too cold. But winter had other plans. Nicholas departed on horseback, riding eastward through Canada, the shortest distance between the two points. Then the snow fell, and it continued to fall until it blocked his path.

Meanwhile, back in Tompkins Township, fifteen-year-old Edward was home alone with no running water, no security alarm and no pantry full of food. A biographer writing about the incident described the cabin as "in the midst of the forest, through whose vastness still roamed bear, wolves and other wild beasts....Indians were not infrequent visitors to the little cabin.... The nearest neighbor was five miles distant."

His father's situation was not much better. The snow was so high in Canada that his horse was unable to bound through it with him on its back. In short, Nicholas was stuck midway between two points in a kind of no-man's-land. To the east of him, his New York family was fatherless, and to the west, his teenage son was alone in the wilderness. But Nicholas was resourceful. He cut down two small trees, turned the trunks into rough-hewn runners and fashioned a homemade sled on which he sat. His innovation worked. The sled rode on top of the snow while the horse pulled it forward. By the time Nicholas arrived home, winter had unleashed its full force. As his son later recalled, "It was finally thought best to not remove the family [from their New York home] at that time." This meant that in Michigan, young Edward was stuck home alone in a dark, cold cabin throughout the winter. One can only wonder what lively conversations ensued between husband and wife about the wisdom of leaving Edward behind.

Flash-forward seven months to April 8. Nicholas, eager to be reunited with Edward, packed a wagon full of household furnishings and provisions and, with thirteen-year-old Richard, set off for Tompkins Township once again. By April 30, they reached the Tompkins farm.

Father and son jumped off the wagon, ran to the cabin and opened the creaky door only to find an empty cabin. Their hearts sank until the shadow of a figure filled the doorway behind them. There, wet and cold and with a stringer of fish in his hand, stood the now sixteen-year-old Edward—a little leaner but very much alive. The survivor, who was equally resourceful, had made it through the winter and was relieved to be reunited with his family at last. The men got the cabin ready and then sent word for the rest of the family, who traveled through Ohio to Detroit, where Edward, Richard and Nicholas were waiting to take them to their new home.

Nicholas went on to be a vital part of Tompkins Township's development, serving as the township supervisor, sheriff and county commissioner, as well as deacon, elder and trustee in the local Presbyterian church. A historian summed up the rest of the Townleys' experiences, and their standing in the community, saying, "The family experienced all the privations of pioneer life, but were rewarded by added comforts as years passed and the hearty respect of those amid whom they labored."[64]

BONES OF A GIANT

History couldn't get more hidden than the buried remnants from the prehistoric past. Such was the legacy of a Tompkins Township farm, where a treasure-trove of historical significance saw the light of day for the first time in eons on January 6, 1955.

The discovery was unearthed when a crane operator for Mead Brothers Excavating was digging marl (lime-rich mud used as fertilizer) from a pond on the property of the Losey family one winter day. All was going well until the mouth of the bucket pulled up something startling from the gooey muck—bones. Giant prehistoric bones, to be exact. What else was entombed in the muck and mire beneath the pond's calm waters? This was, after all, a pond where the owners' unsuspecting children sometimes swam during the summer.

The operator continued to dig and extracted the rest of the jaw, measuring twenty-two inches wide and thirty inches long. Such a strange find demanded expert help. Officials from Michigan State College, now Michigan State University, were called. A paleontologist and other experts arrived to examine the bones and concluded they were from a woolly mammoth—an exciting find since mammoth fossils are less common than mastodons.

Although the animals were similar, mammoths were slightly taller, had more hair, larger ears, longer tusks and different teeth than mastodons. Both

This mastodon skeleton is similar to the woolly mammoth bones dredged from a Tompkins Township pond. *Author's photo, University of Michigan Museum of Natural History.*

were herbivores, and both have been extinct for about ten thousand years. In short, the discovery was exciting. Were there more treasures in the muck?

The excavation, about ten feet below the ground's water table, continued for a couple of weeks, ultimately yielding a lower jaw, two lengths of a tusk, a vertebra, a shoulder blade, leg bones and ankle and leg bone fragments. The bones, known as the Losey Find, were given to Michigan State University in Lansing for further study and research.

The discovery reflects a more mysterious aspect of Michigan's history—a time tens of thousands of years ago, when moving glaciers dug out lakes, ponds and swamps, which were filled by melting snow and natural springs.

Soon, vegetation began to make the area attractive to the North American mastodon and woolly mammoth. The same attraction that lured them here, however, also posed a deadly danger: marshy, swampy ground into which many of the giants got stuck and died. Their murky doom proved to be a blessing for paleontologists, since the marl ended up preserving their ancient bones. Hundreds of mastodon fossils have been found throughout Michigan, while fewer woolly mammoth fossils have been found, rendering the Tompkins Township discovery especially significant. It also proved giants did indeed roam Michigan at one time.[65]

29
Waterloo Township

Fun Facts

- The first settler was Hiram Putnam in 1834. Other early settlers included his brothers, Joseph and Guy Putnam, as well as Abram Croman, Patrick Hubbard, Earl Pierce and Andrew Correll.
- The township was first organized by the name of East Portage in 1836; it adopted its present name in 1846.
- The first sawmill was built by Patrick Hubbard in 1836. With this, he sawed lumber for a gristmill in 1838.
- The first school was built in 1837. Margaret Paddock was the teacher.
- The first post office was established in 1838. Patrick Hubbard was the first postmaster.[66]

From Everts & Stewart Combination Atlas Map of Jackson County, 1874.

THE RAGS-TO-RICHES FARMER

In Michigan's early days, railroads were a double-edged sword that could bless or curse. Towns were built or vacated pending the placement of depots. Fortunes were won or lost based on passengers' spending patterns. Farmers lost livestock or gained customers due to fast-moving locomotives.

One Waterloo Township resident who did more than anyone else to bring the blessings of the rail to his township was Jacob Call (1819–1906). When Call discovered that Grand Trunk Railroad executives were considering laying tracks through Michigan, he sought a depot in Waterloo with single-minded determination. The outcome of his efforts, according to one historian, resulted not only in a depot but also the "flourishing" of a village and the "prosperity" of the surrounding area—no small accomplishment for someone virtually unknown today.

Call, who was born on a farm in Columbia County, New York, moved to Waterloo with his wife, Mary, and their six children in 1855. Although he received little education and was considered a poor man, he put his "strong bodily powers, good health and great energy and determination" to work and ended up prosperous. In time, he owned a 140-acre farm that became "one of the best cultivated and most valuable farms in the...township." He also constructed several buildings on property that he landscaped with various trees, shrubs and an orchard.

But he reserved his "untiring efforts" for persuading railroad executives to lay tracks through Waterloo and "labored with might and main for a station, foreseeing the great advantage to the community." The presence of a track, he anticipated, would bring markets from far away into Waterloo's very midst. Toward this end, he made many sacrifices and "cooperated zealously" with other citizens in Michigan. In "due time, his influence...was rewarded with a station in Munith," resulting in the "subsequent growth of the town." In case Call's efforts in securing the depot were unclear, his biographer further clarified his role: "To him [Jacob Call] more than to any one individual is the above flourishing village indebted for its prosperity, also the surrounding country for its continued growth....In a very large sense he may be considered a benefactor....as he made many sacrifices...and for several years subordinated every other consideration to the one idea of benefiting his fellow men by bringing a market place to their very doors."

According to the book *Michigan Place Names* by Walter Romig, the Grand Trunk Railroad not only laid tracks through Waterloo but also built a depot on the Waterloo farm property owned by Hiram Sutton. The presence of

Wealthy farmer Jacob Call persuaded the railroad to establish a depot in Waterloo Township. *From Everts & Stewart Combination Atlas Map of Jackson County, 1874.*

the depot, originally called Sutton's Crossing, prompted additional changes, including the relocation of the post office, the platting of a new village and new place names. The post office, formerly known as West Portage, was renamed Munith in 1880, and the village took the same name. In a sense, the ripple effect of Call's efforts led to a wave of growth and development that changed the landscape as well as place names.

His biographer wrote, "There has been no disposition on the part of the public to minimize his efforts or in any way to detract from the honors that have crowned his [Call's] labors for the general welfare." Jacob Call, the rags-to-riches farmer whose untiring efforts contributed to the development of the Village of Munith, died in 1906. He was buried at Munith Cemetery.[67]

GERMANY TO WATERLOO

When Katharina Friedericka Ruhl (1811–1884) married Johannes Jacob Seybold (1816–1865) in Wurttemberg, Germany, in 1843, she had no idea she would one day journey 3,662 miles westward across the Atlantic Ocean to the United States—or that the result of her adventure would lead to an enduring legacy for Waterloo Township. It is likely that the thirty-two-year-old widow was simply content to have a partner to help her raise two children in challenging times.

Conditions in Germany around that time were reminiscent of Suzanne Collins's novel *The Hunger Games.* A drought and potato blight had destroyed crops, increased the cost of basic commodities and destabilized a hungry population. In addition, the tradition of passing land ownership to the eldest son had created a huge class of landless sons and non-inheriting daughters.

For these reasons and more, Friedericka and her new husband, whose surname is variously spelled "Seybold," "Seybolt" and "Siebold," immigrated to the United States in 1844. They were not alone. From 1850 through 1870, many German immigrants settled in a region stretching from the New England states to the Great Lakes states, sometimes referred to as the German Belt. So many immigrated, in fact, that German was the second-most popular language in the nation for a time.

The couple's transatlantic voyage was not without danger. Most passengers traveled in steerage class—a lower deck dimly lit by smoky oil lamps and reeking of unemptied chamber pots. Add to this the constant rocking of the enclosure, and it's not surprising that many perished. But Johannes, Friedericka and her two children survived.

They began their experience in America by passing through a New York port and moving westward along the Erie Canal through Buffalo and on to the Great Lakes states. Ultimately, they settled in Waterloo Township, home to a large group of German immigrants. Johannes bought property, built a log cabin and began farming. Historians noted that German families were typically hardworking, close-knit groups whose members were all expected to help out the community, including with fieldwork. That meant Friedericka and her children likely pitched in. Their dedication paid off, and the Seybold farm prospered.

In 1854, the family constructed a new brick two-story home. It was a spacious structure with several rooms, including a hired man's quarters. This level of prosperity and land ownership would not have been possible in their native Germany. The 1860 U.S. census shows a forty-nine-year-old Fredericka Seybold/Seaboard residing in Waterloo with her forty-four-year-old husband, John, and her twenty-one-year-old son, Jacob Ruhl (also spelled "Ruehle"). Likely, her daughter was married and living elsewhere by this time.

In 1862, one year after the Civil War began, Jacob enlisted in Company K, Twentieth Michigan Infantry Regiment. According to military documents, he was five foot five with a light complexion, light hair and gray eyes. Scores of regiments consisted entirely of German Americans—units known for their discipline and daring, according to historians. Around that time, Jacob's surname was changed by accident or by intention from Ruhl/Ruehle to Realy.

He saw action in battles at Antietam, Spottsylvania and Cold Harbor, to name a few. In 1863, he was shot in the hip in Kentucky. Doctors could never remove the bullet, but Jacob recuperated, returned to light service, bullet notwithstanding, and was honorably discharged in 1865. The joy of his return in May of that year was met with sorrow six months later when his stepfather, Johannes Seybold, died at age forty-nine. The hardworking German American was laid to rest at the German Lutheran Cemetery in Waterloo. On his passing, Jacob inherited the farm, where his mother continued to reside.

In 1868, Jacob married Catherine Archenbronn in Waterloo. The couple had seven children. The Realy farm continued to prosper, adding a cider mill and other buildings. In 1884, Friedericka, whose gamble in moving to a new land resulted in prosperity for her family, died at seventy-three

The Realy house, part of the Waterloo Area Farm Museum, Waterloo Township, was built by German immigrants in 1854. *Author's photo.*

years. She was buried beside her husband. When the last Realy descendant living at the farm died in 1960, the family sold the property to the Michigan Department of Natural Resources, which folded the land into the Waterloo State Recreation Area.

In 1962, the Waterloo Area Historical Society traded property it owned elsewhere for three acres of Realy farm property, including the buildings, to establish the Waterloo Farm Museum. In 1973, the farm was listed on the National Register of Historic Places. Today, the museum is a complex of farm buildings open to the public to foster understanding and appreciation of Michigan pioneers. Such a happy ending might have been more than the Realys expected, but it certainly would have made them proud.[68]

Appendix I

Important Firsts

There are many milestones in Jackson County's history. Some made the headlines, though many did not. A comprehensive inventory is too lengthy to list, but below is a sampling of interesting firsts and the dates they occurred.

First Settler's House	Horace Blackman (1829)
First Bridge	Grand River at Trail Street (1830)
First Blacksmith	Josephus Case (1830)
First Black Person in Jackson	Thomas Tryst (or Trist), a blacksmith (1830–35)
First Schoolteacher	Silence D. Blackman (1831)
First Justice of the Peace	William R. DeLand (October 1831)
First Marriage	John T. Durand and Silence D. Blackman (1831)

First Fire Department	Founded after fire at Blackman Tavern (1837)
First Newspaper	*Jacksonburg Sentinel* (1837)
First Abolitionist Newspaper in Michigan	*American Freeman*, founded in Jackson's Public Square (1838–39)
First Prison	North side of downtown (1839)
First Railroad	Michigan Central (1841)
First Jewish Residents	Hirsh, Levy and Wolff families (1842)
First Public Cemetery	Mt. Evergreen Cemetery (1843)
First Black Church	African Methodist Episcopal (1852)
Birthplace of the GOP	Near intersection of Franklin and Second Streets (1854)
First Energy Company	Gas Manufacturing, P.B. Loomis (1857)
First Reading Room (Library Predecessor)	272 West Main Street (Michigan Avenue) (1854)
First Waterworks	Water Street (1870)
First Telephone	Completed by Michigan Central Railroad (1879)
First Black Person Elected in County	Frank Thurman, County Coroner (1880)

APPENDIX 2

MUSEUMS IN JACKSON COUNTY

Treasures from Jackson's history are waiting to be discovered in area museums, from an 1850s farmhouse with a working blacksmith's shop, windmill and granary to an electric interurban railway car that traversed Jackson County's tracks in the early 1900s. Below is a sampling of museums in and around Jackson County. Find one that interests you and then get ready to explore the treasures from Jackson's past.

Cambridge Junction Historic State Park & Walker Tavern Historic Site
Address: 13220 M-50, Brooklyn, 49230
Website: www.Michigan.gov/walkertavern
Phone: (517) 241-0731

Sylvester Walker's farmhouse tavern at Cambridge Junction was a favorite rest stop for travelers in the 1840s. Today, it's part of an eighty-acre state park that showcases three historic buildings and exhibits. The park is operated by the Michigan History Center, Michigan Department of Natural Resources.

Coe House Museum & Grass Lake Area Historical Connection
Address: 371 West Michigan Avenue, Grass Lake, 49240
Website: www.glahc.com
Phone: (517) 522-8324

Built in 1871 in the Tuscan Vernacular style by merchant Henry Vinkle, the Coe House has been renovated to highlight turn-of-the-century life in a small village and features changing exhibits. The house is listed on the Register of Historic Places.

Ella Sharp Museum
Address: 3225 Fourth Street, Jackson, 49203
Website: www.ellasharpmuseum.org
Phone: (517) 787-2320

Art, history and science come together at the Ella Sharp Museum, which showcases art exhibits, historic house tours and a planetarium. Visitors can meet local artists, attend live music performances, visit Ella's farmhouse and stroll the picturesque landscape all in one location.

Hackett Auto Museum
Address: 615 Hupp Avenue, Jackson, 49203
Website: www.hackett-auto-museum.org
Phone: (517) 262-2053

The Hackett Auto Museum showcases Jackson's early automotive history. Visitors will see early cars made in Jackson with educational exhibits and rotating historical items as they relate to Jackson's automotive and worker history.

Hanover-Horton Area Historical Society
Address: 105 Fairview Street, Hanover, 49241
Website: www.conklinreedorganmuseum.org
Phone: (517) 563-8927

This complex includes the Lee Conklin Reed Organ Museum and Heritage Park. The museum, in the 1911 restored Hanover High School building, showcases restored reed organs and classrooms that display local history. Heritage Park, dedicated to rural history, includes an antique farm equipment barn, a maple sugar shack, a sawmill and a woodland walking trail.

Lost Railway Museum
Address: 142 West Michigan Avenue, Grass Lake, 49240
Website: www.lostrailwaymuseum.org
Phone: (517) 522-9500

This museum offers visitors a glimpse of a 1900s-era village before paved streets, cars and buses—a time when the electric interurban railway system was the primary mode of public transportation. It showcases many artifacts, hands-on exhibits and displays, including a restored railcar.

Mann House
Address: 205 Hanover Street, Concord, 49237
Website: www.Michigan.gov/mannhouse
Phone: (517) 241-0731

The Mann House, which reflects Victorian architecture, was once the home of Daniel and Ellen Mann and their two daughters. The museum, operated by the Michigan History Center, Michigan Department of Natural Resources, is furnished with heirlooms, a unique marbleized slate fireplace and treasures from the sisters' travels in Asia.

Michigan Military Heritage Museum
Address: 153 North Union Street, Grass Lake, 49240
Website: www.glahc.com
Phone: (517) 926-6696

This museum highlights Michigan's veterans in peace and war. Exhibits span the Revolutionary War to modern times, including Civil War–era cannons and the nation's most comprehensive World War I combat uniform collection. It also offers a research library.

Michigan Whitetail Hall of Fame Museum
Address: 4220 Willis Road, Grass Lake, 49240
Website: www.facebook.com/deermuseum
Phone: (517) 937-0533

This museum displays more than fifty Boone and Crockett world record buck racks, as well as the country's largest chainsaw and farm implement collection. Visitors also can see and feed live deer throughout the week.

Tompkins Historical Stewart Farm Museum
Address: 10138 Tompkins Road, Rives Junction, 49277
Website: www.tompkinshistorical.org
Phone: (517) 962-3398

The Stewart property features a farmhouse museum, rug looms and blacksmith demonstrations, a replica frontier log cabin, an 1880s schoolhouse, a working windmill and more. Special events include the annual Freedom Festival, featuring a steam engine show, flea market and vintage car show.

Waterloo Farm Museum and Dewey School Museum
Address: 13493 Waterloo-Munith Road, Grass Lake, 49240
Website: www.waterloofarmmuseum.org
Phone: (517) 596-2254

This museum provides a glimpse into nineteenth-century pioneer life. Highlights include a farmhouse built in the 1850s, a restored wooden windmill, a log home, a blacksmith's shop with working forge, a granary and special events. Nearby is the Dewey School Museum, which demonstrates a one-room schoolhouse.

Ye Ole Carriage Shop
Address: 3538 Henderson Road, Spring Arbor, 49283
Website: www.yeolecarriageshop.com
Phone: (517) 414-1733

This museum displays Jackson-made cars and many other classics. Displays include an original Coca-Cola soda shop, a retro kitchen, motorcycles, oil and gas memorabilia, pedal cars and much more. It is designed to give visitors a glimpse of life when Jackson ruled the automobile world.

Notes

Chapter 1

1. DeLand, *History of Jackson County*, 54–95; Deming, *Jackson*, 11–13.

Chapter 2

2. DeLand Family Papers 1842–1913; DeLand Family Papers 1816–1984; DeLand, *History of Jackson County*, 113, 222, 332, 347, 439; Plot records, Mt. Evergreen Cemetery, Jackson.

Chapter 3

3. DeLand, *History of Jackson County*, 108, 142; "Ella Sharp Museum a Brief History," Ella Sharp Museum; *History of Jackson County, Michigan*, Inter-State, 420–22; Michigan Anti-Slavery Newspapers, Charles H. Wright Museum.

Chapter 4

4. DeLand, *History of Jackson County*, 81, 139, 162, 187; Michigan Historical Marker on the property of the First Congregational Church; Leanne Smith, "Peek Through Time: Church's Roots in Jackson Date Back to 1841," *Jackson Citizen Patriot*, August 9, 2010.

Chapter 5

5. DeLand, *History of Jackson County*, 213–14; Michigan Deaths and Burials Index, 1867–1995; U.S. Censuses 1840–1910; Deming, *Jackson*, 19–69; Jackson's Beta Beta Chapter of Delta Kappa Gamma, *Historic Guide to Jackson County*, 24–26.

Chapter 6

6. "History of Second Baptist Church Dates Back to Slavery Days," *Jackson Citizen Patriot*, April 25, 1920; Plot records, Mt. Evergreen Cemetery, Jackson; U.S. Censuses 1850–1910. "Acting on a Vision: Second Baptist Celebrates its 125th Year," *Jackson Citizen Patriot*, July 22, 1990.

Chapter 7

7. "Murder! Mrs. Mary H. Latimer Found Cold in Death in Her Bed Chamber," *Jackson Daily Citizen*, January 25, 1889; "Arrested, R. Irving Latimer in Jail," *Jackson Daily Citizen*, January 27, 1889; "Held For Trial," *Jackson Daily Citizen*, February 1, 1889; "Hunted Down, the Murder Taken, Details of the Capture of Latimer," *Jackson Daily Citizen*, March 29, 1893; "Latimer's Life Begins at 70 as Pardon Wipes Slate Clean," *Detroit Free Press*, May 11, 1935; Plot records, Mt. Evergreen Cemetery, Jackson.

Chapter 8

8. DeLand Family Papers, 1842–1913; DeLand Family Papers 1816–1984; DeLand, *History of Jackson County*, 166–84; "Mass Convention," *American Citizen*, June 28, 1854; "Mass Convention," *American Citizen*, July 5, 1854; "Little White Schoolhouse," National Register of Historic Places Inventory; "Birth of the Republican Party," National Register of Historic Places Inventory; "Ripon to Open G.O.P. Shrine to Public After 75 Years," *Wausau Daily Record-Herald*, October 8, 1932.

Chapter 9

9. *American Citizen*, December 27, 1854; DeLand, *History of Jackson County*, 127, 102–46, 199; "Public Library," *American Citizen*, December 20, 1854; "Ralph Waldo Emerson," *American Citizen*, February 1, 1854; "Young

Men's Association Lecture Course!" *Jackson Daily Citizen*, November 20, 1865; "Young Men's Debate at the Court House," *Jackson Daily Citizen*, December 20, 1854; "History and Facts," Jackson District Library; Leanne Smith, "Peek Through Time: Young Men's Reading Room Leads to 150-Year History of Jackson Library," *Jackson Citizen Patriot*, February 4, 2015.

Chapter 10

10. Merriman Sharp family papers, Ella Sharp Museum Archival Collections, Box 61, folders 6 and 10; Box 62, folders 2 and 6; Box 64, folder 4; Box 66, folder 3; *Jackson Citizen Press*, November 10, 1912; November 11, 1912; Michigan Deaths and Burials Index, 1867–1995; U.S. Censuses 1860–1910; "Ella Sharp Museum a Brief History," Ella Sharp Museum.

Chapter 11

11. DeLand, *History of Jackson County*, 420–21; *History of Jackson County, Michigan,* Inter-State, 762–65; Blackman Township officials.
12. DeLand, *History of Jackson Count*, 80, 136, 212, 248, 349, 432, 461–63; *History of Jackson County, Michigan,* Inter-State, 266; U.S. Censuses 1850–80; Blackman Township officials.
13. DeLand, *History of Jackson County*, 71, 212, 248, 349, 462, 463; *History of Jackson County, Michigan,* Inter-State, 216, 266; U.S. Censuses 1850–80; "Meadow Lark Inn Has a History," *Jackson Citizen Patriot*, July 6, 1924; Leanne Smith, "Peek Through Time: The Blackman Township's Roadhouse Rife with Legends, and Maybe Ghosts," *Jackson Citizen Patriot*, October 29, 2011.

Chapter 12

14. DeLand, *History of Jackson County*, 421–23; *History of Jackson County, Michigan,* Inter-State, 776–824; Columbia Township officials.
15. DeLand, *History of Jackson County,* 314, 422, 423; *History of Jackson County, Michigan,* Inter-State, 788, 799, 815; U.S. Censuses 1840–60; Michigan Deaths and Burials Index, 1867–1995.
16. "Dance Under the Stars: New Ocean Beach Pier, Clark Lake," *Adrian Daily Telegram,* May 25, 1928; "Ocean Beach Pier New to Clark Lake: Open Air Hall for Dancers Offers Opening Features," *Adrian Daily Telegram*, May 26, 1928; "1 Nite Only, Tuesday, Aug. 26, Count Basie," *Adrian Daily Telegram*, August 21, 1941; Leanne Smith, "Peek Through

Time: Clark Lake's Beach Bar Rich in History of Big Bands, Beautiful Views, Good Food," *Jackson Citizen Patriot*, August 20, 2014; Ligibel, *Images of a Michigan Tradition*.

Chapter 13

17. *Combination Atlas Map of Jackson County*, 20–25; DeLand, *History of Jackson County*, 423; *History of Jackson County, Michigan*, Inter-State, 776; Concord Township officials.
18. Clark, *Sex in Education*, 6–19; Michigan Deaths and Burials Index 1867–1995; U.S. Censuses 1850–1900; *Combination Atlas Map*, 23; "Historic Mann House," Michigan Historical Center; Mel Neal, "Dangerous Experiment," *Chronicle*; *Reflections on the Pond*, 213.
19. "Bank Robbers Get $18,000 at Concord," *Kalamazoo Gazette*, November 9, 1917; "Concord Bank Vault Is Blown by Bandits Who Escape with $18,200 Cash," *Jackson Citizen Press*, November 9, 1917; "Concord," *Jackson Sunday Patriot*, November 18, 1917; Ken Wyatt, "Unsolved 1917 Bank Robbery Lit Up Concord with Explosions Heard Miles Away," *Jackson Citizen Patriot*, October 14, 2015.

Chapter 14

20. DeLand, *History of Jackson County*, 423–24; *History of Jackson County, Michigan*, Inter-State, 843–77; Grass Lake Charter Township officials.
21. "A Great Success," *Jackson Citizen Patriot*, May 5, 1903; "Casino Dedication," *Jackson Citizen Patriot*, August 22, 1902; "The Line Complete," *Jackson Citizen*, July 1, 1902; "Wolf Lake," *Jackson Citizen*, July 28, 1902; "Wolf Lake Casino Burns; Woman Has a Narrow Escape: Eight Launches and a Cottage Are Destroyed," *Jackson Citizen Patriot*, September 20, 1913; "Wolf Lake Casino Let," *Jackson Citizen Patriot*, August 1, 1902; "William A. Boland Railroad Builder Expires; Aged 70: Apoplexy Ends Career of Jackson County Financier Known Throughout the United States," *Jackson Citizen Patriot*, September 16, 1918; U.S. Censuses 1850–1910; Leanne Smith, "Peek Through Time: Summer, Fourth of July Have Drawn People to Wolf Lake for More Than a Century," *Jackson Citizen Patriot*, June 27, 2013.
22. *History of Jackson County, Michigan*, Inter-State, 874; Michigan Death Records 1867–1952; U.S. Censuses, 1850–1910; U.S. City Directories, 1822–1995; U.S. Civil War Records, 1861–65.

Chapter 15

23. DeLand, *History of Jackson County*, 424–25; *History of Jackson County, Michigan,* Inter-State, 878–82; Hanover Township officials.
24. DeLand, *History of Jackson County*, 339, 424–25; *Combination Atlas Map*, 23, 885; *History of Jackson County, Michigan,* Inter-State, 878-82; Michigan Death Records, 1867–1952; U.S. Censuses, 1850–1910; U.S. City Directories, 1822–1995.
25. DeLand, *History of Jackson County*, 424–25; *History of Jackson County, Michigan,* Inter-State, 878–82; U.S. Censuses, 1880–1950; U.S. City Directories, 1890–1995; U.S. Find A Grave Index, 1600s–Current; Leanne Smith, "Peek Through Time: As It Turns 100, Hanover School the Focal Point of Village," *Jackson Citizen Patriot*, May 14, 2011.

Chapter 16

26. DeLand, *History of Jackson County*, 425–26; *History of Jackson County, Michigan,* Inter-State, 896–900; Henrietta Township officials.
27. DeLand, *History of Jackson County*, 425–26; *History of Jackson County, Michigan,* Inter-State, 896–900; "John Baptiste Berrard," Quebec, Canada, Vital and Church Records; U.S. Find A Grave Index, 1600s–Current; U.S. Census 1840; U.S. General Land Office Records, 1776–2015; Henrietta Township officials.
28. DeLand, *History of Jackson County*, 546–50; "Patrick Hankerd," *Ingham County Democrat*; U.S Censuses, 1860–1900.

Chapter 17

29. DeLand, *History of Jackson County*, 426; *History of Jackson County, Michigan,* Inter-State, 908–13; Leoni Township officials.
30. DeLand, *History of Jackson County*, 288; *History of Jackson County, Michigan,* Inter-State, 328; Seymour Boughton Treadwell Papers, Bentley Historical Library; U.S. Censuses, 1830–60.
31. DeLand, *History of Jackson County*, 153–60; *History of Jackson County, Michigan,* Inter-State, 446–52; Ken Wyatt, "Peek Through Time: Railroads That Helped Jackson County Grow Also Infuriated Local Farmers," *Jackson Citizen Patriot*, February 15, 2012.

Chapter 18

32. DeLand, *History of Jackson County*, 427–28; *History of Jackson County, Michigan,* Inter-State, 937–38; Liberty Township officials.
33. DeLand, *History of Jackson County*, 427; U.S. Homestead and Cash Entry Patents, Pre-1908; *History of Jackson County, Michigan,* Inter-State, 952–54; U.S. Censuses, 1830–70; U.S. Find A Grave Index, 1600s–Current.
34. U.S. Appointments of Postmasters, 1832–1971; U.S. Censuses, 1850–80; U.S. Find a Grave Index, 1600s–Current; South Jackson Community Church staff and historian.

Chapter 19

35. DeLand, *History of Jackson County*, 428; *History of Jackson County, Michigan,* Inter-State, 959–61; Napoleon Township officials.
36. DeLand, *History of Jackson County*, 394; *History of Jackson County, Michigan,* Inter-State, 969; U.S. Censuses, 1850–1900; U.S. Civil War Soldier Records and Profiles, 1861–65; U.S. Appointments of Postmasters, 1832–1971; U.S. College Student Lists, 1763–1924; U.S. Find A Grave Index, 1600s–Current; Dorwart, "Essential Civil War Curriculum"; "Battle of Fredericksburg," History; "Battle of Vicksburg," History.
37. "Death of an Old Settler," *American Citizen*, April 15, 1863; Haviland, *Woman's Life-Work*, 182–84; U.S. Censuses 1850–60; U.S. Find A Grave Index, 1600s–Current; Bill Markley, "Napoleon Couple Live in House on Land Granted by Jackson," *Jackson Citizen Patriot*, February 27, 1946; Mull, *Underground Railroad*, 118; Nellie Blair Greene, "Historic Homes of Jackson County, No. 5—The Palmer House," *Jackson Citizen Patriot*, August 23, 1924.

Chapter 20

38. DeLand, *History of Jackson County*, 428–29; *History of Jackson County, Michigan,* Inter-State, 959–61; Norvell Township officials.
39. Haviland, *Woman's Life-Work*, 67–70; Michigan Pioneer and Historical Society Collections, Vol. 26, 644; *Portrait and Biographical Album of Jackson County*, 445–47; U.S. Censuses, 1840–70; U.S. Find A Grave Index, 1600s–Current.
40. DeLand, *History of Jackson County*, 135; *History of Jackson County, Michigan,* Inter-State, 966–67; U.S. Censuses, 1850–90; U.S. Find A Grave Index, 1600s–Current.

Chapter 21

41. DeLand, *History of Jackson County*, 429–30; *History of Jackson County, Michigan,* Inter-State, 1,007–8; Parma Township officials.
42. DeLand, *History of Jackson County*, 347; Hass, *Michigan's Crossroads to Freedom*, 37–38; Nellie Blair Greene, "Historic Jackson County No. 14, Quakertown, Parma," *Jackson Tribune*, November 8, 1929.
43. *Portrait and Biographical Album of Jackson County*, 529–530; U.S. Censuses, 1850–80; U.S. Find a Grave Index, 1600s–Current.

Chapter 22

44. DeLand, *History of Jackson County*, 430–32; *History of Jackson County, Michigan,* Inter-State, 1,023–25; Pulaski Township officials.
45. *Combination Atlas Map,* 115; DeLand, *History of Jackson County*, 431; *History of Jackson County, Michigan,* Inter-State, 1,031; U.S. Censuses, 1850–90; U.S. Find A Grave Index, 1600s–Current; "Postmasters in the Mid-19th Century," United States Postal Service; *Reflections on the Pond*; Longfellow, "Transportation in America's Postal System."
46. DeLand, *History of Jackson County*, 80, 254, 256, 340, 431–32; Bernard, *American Biographical History*, 135–36; *History of Jackson County, Michigan,* Inter-State, 1,023; U.S. Censuses, 1850–70; Cunningham, *Spring Arbor Township*; Ken Wyatt, "Peek Through Time: Swain's Lake History Tied to Early Settler, Decades of Enjoyable Summer Days," *Jackson Citizen Patriot*, July 19, 2012.

Chapter 23

47. DeLand, *History of Jackson County*, 432–33; *History of Jackson County, Michigan,* Inter-State, 1,032–33; Rives Township officials.
48. DeLand, *History of Jackson County*, 623–25; *History of Jackson County, Michigan,* Inter-State, 1,035; U.S. Censuses, 1850–1900; U.S. Find A Grave Index, 1600s–Current; "20 Michigan Agriculture Facts," Pure Michigan.
49. Morgan, "They Went"; Ken Wyatt, "Peek Through Time: Michigan's Terminus, Which Includes Rives Township, Is an Intriguing Story," *Jackson Citizen Patriot*, December 31, 2010; "USPLS Survey," Michigan State University.

Chapter 24

50. DeLand, *History of Jackson County*, 433–34; *History of Jackson County, Michigan,* Inter-State, 1,050; Sandstone Charter Township officials.
51. DeLand, *History of Jackson County*, 433–34; *History of Jackson County, Michigan,* Inter-State, 1,050; U.S. Censuses, 1850–70; Ken Wyatt, "Peek Through Time: Barry, Michigan: The Town Time Forgot," *Jackson Citizen Patriot*, September 17, 2011; Romig, *Michigan Place Names*, 499.
52. *Combination Atlas Map*, 73, 444–45; U.S. Censuses 1840–1910; U.S. Find A Grave Index, 1600s–Current.

Chapter 25

53. DeLand, *History of Jackson County*, 434–35; *History of Jackson County, Michigan,* Inter-State, 1,059–61; Spring Arbor Township officials.
54. DeLand, *History of Jackson County*, 433–34; *History of Jackson County, Michigan, Inter-State*, 1,050; Cunningham, *Spring Arbor Township*, 169–73; Spring Arbor FMC. "Spring Arbor Free Methodist Church: The Short Story."
55. *Combination Atlas Map*, 805–7; U.S. Censuses, 1850–1900; Cunningham, *Spring Arbor Township*, 56–57; U.S. Find A Grave Index, 1600s–Current.

Chapter 26

56. Joy, *Pioneer History of Springport*; DeLand, *History of Jackson County*, 435; *History of Jackson County, Michigan,* Inter-State, 1,078–79; Springport Township officials.
57. U.S. Appointments of Postmasters, 1832–1971; DeLand, *History of Jackson County*, 668–71; U.S. Censuses, 1840–60; U.S. Find A Grave Index, 1600s–Current.
58. Joy, *Pioneer History of Springport Township*; U.S. Censuses, 1850–1910; U.S. Civil War Soldier Records and Profiles, 1861–65; Find A Grave Index, 1600s–Current.

Chapter 27

59. DeLand, *History of Jackson County*, 435–36; *History of Jackson County, Michigan,* Inter-State, 1,098; Summit Township officials.
60. "Mrs. Roosevelt in Seclusion Near Here: First Lady Is Brown's Lake Cottage Guest," *Jackson Citizen Patriot*, September 9, 1935.

61. "Immense Crowd at Hague Park," *Jackson Citizen Patriot*, July 5, 1912; Miller and Bennett, *Threads of Vandercook*, 148–52; Leanne Smith, "Peek Through Time: Jack Rabbit, Warm Summer Days Drew Thousands to Vandercook Lake's Hague Park," *Jackson Citizen Patriot*, May 10, 2012.
62. "The Cascades," Jackson County Parks; "Magic Fountain of Montjuic," Tourist Guide Barcelona.

Chapter 28

63. DeLand, *History of Jackson County*, 435–36; *History of Jackson County, Michigan*, Inter-State, 1,098; Tompkins Township officials.
64. DeLand, *History of Jackson County*, 1,009–11; *History of Jackson County, Michigan*, Inter-State, 1,116–17; *Portrait and Biographical Album*, 710–11, 822–24; U.S. Censuses, 1830–1900.
65. Bob McGregor, "Discovery on Tompkins Farm Opens Page in County History," *Jackson Citizen Patriot*, January 7, 1955; Hall, "Scientists, Visitors Converge"; "Pre-Historic Bones Found on Vern Losey Farm," *Springport Signal*, January 12, 1955; Leanne Smith, "Peek Through Time: In 1955, Wooly Mammoth Bones Found on Tompkins Township Farm," *Jackson Citizen Patriot*, January 16, 2010.

Chapter 29

66. DeLand, *History of Jackson County*, 436; *History of Jackson County, Michigan*, Inter-State, 1,132–33; Waterloo Township officials.
67. DeLand, *History of Jackson County*, 1,067–70; *Combination Atlas Map*, 56; *History of Jackson County, Michigan*, Inter-State, 1,137; U.S. Censuses, 1866–1900.
68. Michigan Marriage Records, 1867–1952; Michigan Death Records, 1867–1952; Michigan, Wills and Probate Records, 1784–1980; U.S. Censuses, 1850–1910; U.S. Civil War Pension Index, 1861–65; U.S. Civil War Soldier Records and Profiles, 1861–65; "Waterloo Farm Museum," Experience Jackson.

Selected Bibliography

Newspapers

Adrian Daily Telegram. 1928–41.
American Citizen (Jackson, MI). 1849–64.
American Freeman (Jackson, MI). 1839–40.
Hall, Neil. "Scientists, Visitors Converge on Mammoth Discovery." *State Journal*, January 7, 1955.
Ingham County Democrat. "Patrick Hankerd." September 27, 1991.
Jackson Citizen Patriot. 1888–2017.
Jacksonburg Sentinel. April 22, 1837.
Jackson Sunday Patriot, 1917.
Kalamazoo Gazette. "Bank Robbers Get $18,000 at Concord." November 9, 1917.
Michigan Freeman. September 25, 1839; October 21, 1840.
Springport Signal. "Pre-Historic Bones Found on Vern Losey Farm." January 12, 1955.
Wausau (WI) Daily Record-Herald. "Ripon to Open G.O.P. Shrine to Public After 75 Years." October 8, 1932.

Print Materials

Bernard, F.A. *American Biographical History of Eminent and Self-Made Men*. Michigan Volume. Cincinnati, OH: Western Biographical Publishing Co., 1878.
Clark, Edward H. *Sex in Education: A Fair Chance for Girls*. Boston: Houghton Mifflin, 1884.

Combination Atlas Map of Jackson County, Michigan/Compiled, drawn and published from personal examinations and surveys. Chicago: Everts & Stewart, 1874.

Crandall, Andrew W. *The Early History of the Republican Party 1854–56.* Gloucester, MA: Peter Smith, 1960.

Cunningham, Beverly. *Spring Arbor Township: 1830–2013.* Spring Arbor, MI: Saltbox Press, 2013.

"A Dangerous Experiment." *Chronicle* 42, no. 3 (Fall 2019).

DeLand, Charles Victor. *History of Jackson County, Michigan: Embracing a Concise Review of its Early Settlement, Industrial Development and Present Conditions, Together with interesting Reminiscences.* Chicago: B.F. Bowen, 1903.

Deming, Brian. *Jackson: An Illustrated History.* Woodland Hills, CA: Windsor Publications Inc., 1984.

Fairbanks, Mrs. A.W., ed. *Emma Willard and Her Pupils; Or, Fifty Years of Troy Female Seminary, 1822–1872.* New York: N.p., 1898.

Hass, Linda. *Michigan's Crossroads to Freedom: The Underground Railroad in Jackson County.* St. Petersburg, FL: Booklocker.com, 2017.

Haviland, Laura S. Laura Haviland Papers. 1868–1933. Bentley Historical Library. University of Michigan, Ann Arbor.

———. *A Woman's Life-Work: Labors and Experiences.* London: Forgotten Books, 2008. First published 1882 by Walden and Stowe for the author (Cincinnati, OH).

History of Jackson County, Michigan. Chicago: Interstate Publishing, 1881.

Jackson's Beta Beta Chapter of Delta Kappa Gamma and the Jackson Branch of the American Association of University Women. *Historic Guide to Jackson County.* Self-published, Creative Graphics, 2004.

Joy, Ben A. *Pioneer History of Springport Township.* Springport, MI: *Springport Signal*, 1910.

Ligibel, Ted J. *Clark Lake: Images of a Michigan Tradition.* Clark Lake, MI: Clark Lake Historical Preservation Committee, 1991.

Michigan Pioneer and Historical Society. *Historical Collections.* Lansing: Michigan State Historical Society, Michigan Historical Commission, various dates.

Miller, Chuck, and Ron Bennett. *The Threads of Vandercook.* Vandercook Lake, MI: Creative Graphics, 2011.

Mull, Carol E. *The Underground Railroad in Michigan.* Jerfferson, NC: McFarland & Company, 2010.

Portrait and Biographical Album of Jackson County, Michigan, Containing Full Page Portraits and Biographical Sketches of Prominent and Representative Citizens of the County, Together with Portraits and Biographies of All the Governors of the State, and of the Presidents of the United States. Chicago: Chapman Bros., 1890.

Reflections on the Pond. Brooklyn, MI: Concord Heritage Association, 1976.

Romig, Walter. *Michigan Place Names: The History of the Founding and the Naming of More Than Five Thousand Past and Present Michigan Communities.* Detroit, MI: Wayne State University Press, 1986.

Thomas, James M., ed. *History of Jackson County, Michigan: Together with Sketches of its Cities, Villages and Townships, Jackson City Directory* and *Business Advertiser for 1867 & 1868.* Jackson, MI: Carlton & Van Antwerp Printers, 1867.

Historical Collections and Pamphlets

DeLand Family Papers 1842–1913. Bentley Historical Library. University of Michigan, Ann Arbor.

DeLand Family Papers 1816–1984. Burton Historical Collection. Detroit Public Library, Detroit, MI.

"Historic Mann House." Michigan Historical Center Field Site Tour Manual. Michigan Anti-Slavery Newspapers. Charles H. Wright Museum of African American History, Detroit, MI.

McGee, Melville. "Early Days of Concord, Jackson County Michigan." *Michigan Pioneer Collections.* Vol. 21 (1892).

Seymour Boughton Treadwell Papers. Bentley Historical Library. University of Michigan, Ann Arbor.

Public Records

"Birth of the Republican Party Under the Oaks." National Register of Historic Places Inventory—Nomination Form. United States Department of the Interior National Park Service.

Civil War Soldier Records and Profiles, 1861–65.

"John Baptiste Berrard." Quebec, Canada, Vital and Church records, 1621–1928

"Little White Schoolhouse: Birthplace of the Republican Party." National Register of Historic Places Inventory—Nomination Form. United States Department of the Interior National Park Service.

Michigan Deaths and Burials Index, 1867–1995.

Michigan Marriage Records, 1867–1952.

Michigan, Wills and Probate Records, 1784–1980.

Quebec, Canada Vital and Church Records, 1621–1928.

U.S. Appointments of Postmasters, 1832–1971.

U.S. Censuses, 1840–1910.

U.S. City Directories, 1822–1995.

U.S. Civil War Pension Index: General Index to Pension Files, 1861–65.

U.S. Civil War Records, 1861–65.
U.S. Civil War Soldier Records and Profiles, 1861–65.
U.S. College Student Lists, 1763–1924.
U.S. Find A Grave Index, 1600s–Current.
U.S. General Land Office Records 1776–2015.
U.S. Homestead and Cash Entry Patents, Pre-1908.

Internet Sources

"Battle of Fredericksburg." History. Updated December 11, 2019. https://www.history.com/topics/american-civil-war/battle-of-fredericksburg.

"The Cascades (also known as the Cascade Falls)." Jackson County Parks. https://www.co.jackson.mi.us/1298/The-Cascades.

Dorwart, Dr. Bonnie Brice. "Civil War Medicine." Essential Civil War Curriculum. https://www.essentialcivilwarcurriculum.com/civil-war-medicine.html.

"Ella Sharp Museum a Brief History." Ella Sharp Museum. https://ellasharpmuseum.org/about.

"Experience Jackson's Prison History." Experience Jackson. https://www.experiencejackson.com/things-to-do/historic-jackson/prison-history.

"History and Facts." Jackson District Library. http://myjdl.com/history-and-facts.

"Kazimierz Pulaski." *Encyclopedia Britannica*. https://www.britannica.com/biography/Kazimierz-Pulaski.

Longfellow, Rickie. "Transportation in America's Postal System." Highway History. Updated June 27, 2017. https://www.fhwa.dot.gov/infrastructure/back0304.cfm.

"The Magic Fountain of Montjuic, Barcelona Guide." Tourist Guide Barcelona. https://www.barcelona-tourist-guide.com/en/albums-en/magic-fountains-montjuic/index.html.

"Mann House." Pure Michigan. https://www.michigan.org/property/mann-house.

Morgan, Deidra. "They Went Where Only Indians Had Been." *Bittersweet* 10, no. 2 (Winter 1982). https://thelibrary.org/lochist/periodicals/bittersweet/wi82e.htm.

MSU Department of Geography. "USPLS Survey." Michigan State University. http://geo.msu.edu/extra/geogmich/Survey.html.

"Postmasters in the Mid-19th Century." United States Postal Service. https://about.usps.com.

"Siege of Vicksburg." History. Updated April 12, 2020. https://www.history.com/topics/american-civil-war/vicksburg-campaign.

"South Jackson Community Church History." South Jackson Community Church. https://www.southjacksoncommunitychurch.org/history.

Spring Arbor FMC. "Spring Arbor Free Methodist Church: The Short Story." Uploaded August 15, 2011. Video, 15:19. https://vimeo.com/27752809.

"20 Michigan Agriculture Facts You Might Not Have Known." Pure Michigan. https://www.michigan.org.

"Waterloo Farm Museum." Waterloo Farm Museum. http://waterloofarmmuseum.org/

"Waterloo Farm Museum and Dewey School Museum." Experience Jackson. https://www.experiencejackson.com/business/waterloo-farm-museum-and-dewey-school-museum.

About the Author

Courtesy Meadow Lace Photography.

Linda Hass is a Jackson-based author/researcher/presenter who specializes in local history. Linda, who has a master's degree in journalism from Michigan State University, has authored two previous books: *Michigan's Crossroads to Freedom* and *Hidden in Plain Sight*. She also researched and applied for three historical distinctions in Jackson: the Michigan State Historical Marker in Bucky Harris Park honoring abolitionist activities that occurred there, the Michigan State Historical Marker in Mt. Evergreen Cemetery honoring Underground Railroad activists buried there and a National Park Service certificate listing Mt. Evergreen Cemetery in the National Underground Railroad Network to Freedom. (For more information, see jacksonmiundergroundrailroad.com.) When not giving tours, exploring cemeteries or traveling to archives and museums, Linda and her husband, Ed, enjoy long walks on Jackson's Falling Waters Trail.